1-6-67

THE GHETTO OF
INDIFFERENCE

THE GHETTO OF INDIFFERENCE

Thomas J. Mullen

ABINGDON PRESS | NASHVILLE
NEW YORK

Library of Congress Catalog Card Number: 66-14994

SET UP, PRINTED, AND BOUND BY THE
PARTHENON PRESS, AT NASHVILLE,
TENNESSEE, UNITED STATES OF AMERICA

1388571

**TO THE FRIENDS
OF NEW CASTLE**

PREFACE

Books about the poor, the Negro, and the residents of "other America" are usually written by persons who are "experts" in this area. A Martin Luther King can write about the dilemmas of being a Negro, and we have every reason to listen to what he says because he speaks from inside the problem. Michael Harrington can tell of the strange world of the poverty-stricken with authority because, as a sociologist and a concerned human being, he knows intellectually and intimately the world about which he writes. It would be presumptuous for one who is neither a sociologist nor a refugee from the slum world to pretend to be an expert about the inside of the problems of poverty and race.

However, this book is not really about the inside of these huge problems, except through incidental references to them. Rather, it is concerned with people about whom the author *is* something of an expert—the white, Anglo-Saxon, middle-class persons who compose the vast majority of the Protestant churches. I do live on the inside of this world, and I am thoroughly familiar with the orientation of WASP-land. I have been, and to some extent still am, a part of their ghetto, and my qualifications for WASP membership are genuine and nearly complete.

I come from a middle-class home in which my father and mother provided us with a good living from a grocery store or a farm or a small business. Early I learned the virtues of hard work and decent living. My blood lines are about as Anglo-Saxon as they can get, representing Scotch, Irish, and German ancestry. I am pastor of a medium-sized Protestant church in a medium-sized midwestern community, a member (though inactive) of the Masonic Lodge, and a registered (though somewhat disillusioned) Republican. The WASPs are my people, and I am one of them.

Unlike many of that great group of middle-class Protestants, however, others have led me by the hand across the tracks to other ghettos where live the invisible Americans about whom I had known only from books and college courses. There have been enough moments of escape to inspire this book, for it is apparent that the church of Jesus Christ, in its local chapters, will never be true to the gospel until it escapes from its bonds of provincialism and indifference. Hopefully, it is not too late for this to happen, but we WASPs have no time to waste for the walls between the other America and ourselves grow taller each passing day.

Special thanks are due William Meuhl of Yale Divinity School who provided the germ of the idea for the concluding parable in the final chapter. He may have long ago forgotten that sermon, but this student was deeply moved by it. Public thanks is due my wife, Nancy, who was chief critic for the manuscript and is a prime example of "Christian schizophrenia" (see chap. 4). Appreciation is in order, also, to Mrs. Earl Sheppard, our long-suffering church secretary who typed the entire manuscript and managed the difficult translation of inserts, deletions, and awkward sentences into something resembling the English language.

Finally, however, many words of appreciation must be directed toward the members of the New Castle Friends Meeting who have inspired my best literary efforts and tolerated my worst. They are an exceptional group of WASPs who, collectively and individually, have built many bridges between the world of the haves and the have-nots. Because of their openness to new ideas, their willingness to experiment, and their ability to forgive, they have made the task of being their pastor both a challenge and a joy.

It is with sincere respect and deep affection that this book is dedicated to them.

TOM MULLEN

CONTENTS

THE HAVES AND
THE HAVE-NOTS

1

Thousands of Protestants live in a ghetto. Its walls are high, and they are made of the stuff of culture, custom, race, and class. The people who live in this small world are the WASPs—the white, Anglo-Saxon Protestants of the middle class—and they have little contact with those outside their ghetto.

In recent years the word "WASP" has come to be a shorthand form to identify the average white Christian in rural and suburban Protestant churches. Partly because of the unusual combination of letters which suggest that he is some kind of bug, the term "WASP" has seemed to ridicule this large, hard-core Christian group. This implication is not really fair because the WASPs have many virtues and from their number have come many truly dedicated Christians. In short, WASP is neither a negative nor a positive term but merely a descriptive one, a term used to designate the good, solid, employed, honest, thrifty folk who compose the bulk of the membership of our churches. Not all WASPs are active members by any means, and some of the faults which are attributed to the Protestant churches they populate are exemplified by many persons who are enrolled members in name only. However, in this general way they can be identified and, in fact, if you, gentle reader, are a Methodist, Presbyterian, Baptist, or a member of another mainline Protestant church, chances are you are one of them.

The WASPs do not live in a ghetto because they have been forced to do so. It is a ghetto of their own choosing, their own making, and their own thinking. More often than not, they are not even aware of their own condition, for the provincial world in which they live is one of indifference and unconcern. If we think of a ghetto as a restricted area, a place where people live and suffer because their world is small and closes in upon them, a place where the experience of living is limited, then it is accurate to say that WASPs live in such a psychological environment.

Illustrations of this fact are legion. We are all familiar with the charge—the accurate charge, we might add—that Protestant churches are the most segregated institutions in a community, and that 11 o'clock on Sunday morning is the most segregated hour of the week. It is not uncommon to find large churches in large cities with hundreds of members who do not have even a single person who is also a member of a labor union.

In one medium-sized northern community it had not been possible for years for a Negro man or boy to get his hair cut in his own city. The male members of the nonwhite population had traveled fifteen or twenty miles to other cities (where there were Negro barbers) to get their hair cut. Yet, in this city there are, at last count, forty-eight white church congregations, and only

14

a handful of their members were even *aware* that this degrading practice had been going on for years.

Few of the smiling middle-class folk who greet the "trick-or-treaters" on Halloween and cheerfully put candy and apples in their sacks know that many of those masked children are not just playing a sweet and traditional game. They are unaware that many of them had been sent out with explicit instructions from their parents to return home only when their bags had been completely filled to overflowing, for their receipts will be the primary source of delicacies for the entire family for many days to come. Interestingly, the favorite costume of these children is the hobo outfit, the components for which are easily accessible.

That which is either a kind of social occasion or a genuine money-raising effort for most middle-class Protestants—the rummage sale—is the primary way in which many families clothe their children and themselves. Indeed, without even knowing it, the WASPS have been providing a crucial service for some persons in all kinds and sizes of communities who possibly never, in their entire lives, have bought clothes first hand in a retail store. True, many frugal middle-class Christians pick up bargains at a rummage sale now and then, but the difference is they don't *have* to buy there.

Only a few hospital chaplains or an occasional social worker are familiar with the attitude of deep resentment, even hatred, or certainly suspicion which the have-nots of a city feel toward the haves. They do not even know that they represent to many poor and frustrated souls a world of shop owners, bosses, and managers who have exploited them in the past and probably will do so in the future. Much of this resentment is unjustified and unfair, but it is there, and the point is that relatively few white, Anglo-Saxon, middle-class Protestants even know it exists.

Negroes interviewed at a midwestern liberal arts college agreed that many of their fellow white students were simply victims of "plain ignorance." They felt that, especially among freshmen, a sheltered home life and the former lack of any contact with Negroes had led to misconceptions about them. "People like this aren't really prejudiced," one Negro commented, *"They are merely ignorant, coming as they do from the provincial environment of middle-class suburbia."* (Italics mine.)

There is, in short, a wide and deep gap which separates the haves from the have-nots, almost as if one part of America lived in a slum for the poor and disenfranchised while another part lived in a psychological ghetto that blinds it to persons outside its walls. The sociologists and the theologians discovered a long time ago [1] that Protestant Christianity is segmented more along social, economic, and racial lines than along theological ones. Even as a boy growing up in rural

[1] See, for example, H. Richard Niebuhr's classic works, *The Social Sources of Denominationalism* or *Christ and Culture.* Other significant and more recent studies include *Treasure in Earthen Vessels* by James Gustafson and Gibson Winter's *The Suburban Captivity of the Churches.* There are many others.

Indiana, this writer noted obvious indications that such was the case. In our town there were three Protestant churches, and it was common knowledge that the well-to-do went to the Presbyterian Church, the poorer people to the Methodist Church, and the other church —a Disciples of Christ congregation—got its members primarily from those people who were too poor to be Presbyterians and too proud to be Methodists.

This situation is humorous and certainly exaggerated, but it was not particularly destructive, either for the churches or for the community as a whole. However, as America has grown and as rural America diminishes in size and influence, the problem of the separation of the haves from the have-nots has become larger and no longer is very funny—at least to the have-nots. Michael Harrington in his book, *The Other America,* describes the plight of millions of people whose condition is virtually unknown to the WASPs.[2]

We have always had the poor with us, as the "Good Book" says, but now they are "with" us in theory but certainly not in fact. Harrington puts it this way:

[2] The definition of the "have-nots" which we are using in this book roughly resembles the categories discussed by Michael Harrington in *The Other America* (Baltimore: Penguin Books, 1962). They include "the rejects" (those perpetually unemployed), the rural poor, the Negro, the aged poor, and transient groups such as migrant laborers. Many Negroes, of course, have achieved middle-class status economically, but we are retaining the problem of civil rights as a part of our discussion of the "have-nots" because the two are so closely allied. Also, many Negroes who can afford a better life are still denied one because of their color.

17

The very development of American society is creating a new kind of blindness about poverty. The poor are increasingly slipping out of the very experience and consciousness of the nation.

If the middle class never did like ugliness and poverty, it was at least aware of them. "Across the tracks" was not a very long way to go. There were forays into slums at Christmas time; there were the charitable organizations that brought contact with the poor. Occasionally, almost everyone passed through the Negro ghetto or the blocks of tenements, if only to get downtown to work or to entertainment.

Now the American city has been transformed. The poor still inhabit the miserable housing in the central area, but they are increasingly isolated from contact with, or sight of, anybody else. Middle-class women coming in from Suburbia on a rare trip may catch the merest glimpse of the other America on the way to an evening at the theater, but their children are segregated in suburban schools. The business or professional man may drive along the fringes of slums in a car or bus, but it is not an important experience to him. The failures, the unskilled, the disabled, the aged, and the minorities are right there, across the tracks, where they have always been. But hardly anyone else is.[3]

Harrington speaks, obviously, of the middle class which lives in or around large cities, but the ghetto of the WASPs looms even larger in our imagination if we add to it the medium-sized cities, the towns, and the hamlets where there may not even be any tracks across which the poor may live. Yet, here is where grass-roots

[3] *The Other America,* pp. 11-12.

18

Protestantism still dwells, and its members may not have even the minimal contact of which Harrington speaks.

Not only are the haves usually unaware of the have-nots and the lives they lead, frequently they are not aware of their own status as members of an affluent society. Many of us lived and suffered through the great depression. Many of us worked our way through college. We have mortgages on our homes, and we find money does not grow on trees. When we read statistics about the forty or fifty million Americans who are at the poverty levels of the economy, we are tempted to check the figures to see if *our* names have been included. The psychological gap between the two Americas is widened because we do not really know how very much better off most middle-class Protestants are than the have-nots.

We can see this very quickly by asking ourselves some simple questions. How many members of the congregation to which we belong have ever been on relief? How many have ever visited the township trustee to seek some food to carry them through a hard time? On Mother's Day, when we award the traditional potted plants to the youngest and oldest mothers, are there any ladies in competition who wait anxiously each month for their Aid to Dependent Children checks? Which of the members of your church were ever refused service in a restaurant because of race or color? As the white Protestants move to the suburbs, the have-nots stay where they are. The Negroes remain in their

19

ghettos, the poor in their slums, the aged in their crummy apartments, and the migrants in their shacks.

The ghetto of indifference in which we WASPs live is kept isolated by our churches as well as by our cultural and economic differences. That local churches are seldom aware of the have-nots is evident from the kinds of programs and interests they promote. Beginning with Sunday school materials which universally, until very recently, pictured all God's children as neatly dressed, freshly scrubbed, and pale-faced, and carrying through the activities of the men's group and the women's missionary society, they show a naïveté about the other America which has to be studied, weekly, to be believed.

Why has the emphasis on "peace of mind" been so well received among Protestants in this part of the twentieth century? It is because it seems to be a reasonable attempt to meet middle-class needs. After all, the concerns of the middle-class Christians are not with basic and fundamental matters—hunger, nakedness, discrimination, or poverty. Our concerns, yours and mine, are with such matters as how to deal with tension-producing circumstances between employer and employee, depression over the loss of a promotion, or anxieties over our youth who seem to have too much time on their hands. We fret over the pressures we feel on our jobs or the degree of acceptance we receive from other leaders in the lonely crowd. Among the anxieties which encouraged the rise of positive thinking and other forms of religious aspirin-taking have been several legitimate

20

concerns. Grief from personal loss, for example, knows no class or color. A sense of failure is not limited just to the poverty-stricken. There are, obviously, a great many genuine problems which plague WASPs, and it is right that local churches try to meet them head on.

However, our preoccupation with positive thinking as a solution to our needs also indicates our psychological separation from the have-nots. A Negro man can think as positively as he wants, and he is still going to have trouble buying a house outside his ghetto. A mother who sees her children going to bed hungry several nights a week is anxious and disturbed, but cheerful optimism is scarcely the solution to her frustration. The discouragement a high school girl feels because she didn't get accepted by her first choice of college, among the several to which she applied, has little to do with the problem of the girl who may *want* to get pregnant in order to get away from a terrible home environment. The slogan, "Find Strength for Your Life, Go to Church This Sunday," is ludicrous advice to the perpetually unemployed. We accept the fact in our local churches that the world of the have-nots is foreign to it by virtue of the kind of gospel we preach.

Another example of the separation we recognize implicitly is our preoccupation with statistical success. Several books have already been written deploring the fact that our churches are more interested in membership totals than commitment, or that to be a successful church means to build a new building as soon as possible. However, like the weather, this is a problem often discussed but seldom solved, at least at the local level.

The reason it is seldom solved is that this is the predominant attitude of middle-class people. You build a nice house (or church) and you keep it in good repair. Or you save until you can afford (or have enough members) to build a bigger and better one (house or church). The churchly concerns are analogous to the daily concerns of business and everyday life. How often we have heard the local church criticized for being just like the Rotary Club or the Masonic Lodge, when it has a multitude of reasons (its members!) for being that way. After all, there are very few service club members or lodge members or women's club members who have ever spent as many as six consecutive hours in a slum building—except possibly to collect the rent. Why should these persons be expected, suddenly, to change their thinking because they may stroll through the doors of a church once a week or less often?

There are extreme examples of this attitude which merely indicate how success-oriented Protestants can become as they grow in wisdom and stature and in favor with the First National Bank. Clyde Reid, writing in *The Christian Century,* exposed some interesting illustrations of how some truly "successful" congregations think and act.

In New York City a prominent church is spending $350,-000 to add carvings and statues to the Gothic facade of its building. From sidewalk level many of the statues, which represent saints and other personages in Christian history, will scarcely be discernible. . . .

A few blocks away another "prestige" church is spending $850,000 to restore and renovate the stone facade of its building and to install a new entrance and vestibule. Explains the architect: "We want the church to have a Fifth avenue look."

In a recent issue of the *New York Times* a historic local church announced plans to add, at a cost of $350,000, a two-story addition to contain "a sacristy, choir rooms, dressing rooms for assistants at the services and a meeting hall where historical material from the church's past can be displayed." . . .

Still another New York church recently announced (pridefully) that it is spending $125,000 to *improve* its pipe organ. And a large suburban church has a new lounge for its women's society, equipped (at a cost of $10,000) with thick carpet, marble-topped tables and other "elegant" furnishings.[4]

Not at all surprisingly, several letters to the editor in later issues and a number of private comments by pastors who discussed the article revealed their disagreement with Reid's point, primarily on the ground that the church was a vessel to express the beauty and harmony of God through architecture and physical structure. Once again, however, such concerns are scarcely of interest to the have-nots, and Reid's point is well taken when he comments: "A news item reported that the

[4] "Let's Stop Building Cathedrals!" p. 797. Copyright 1964 Christian Century Foundation. Reprinted by permission from the June 17, 1964 issue of *The Christian Century*.

state of New York will spend $60,000 to open a clinic for alcoholics in nearby Westchester county—on a one-year experimental basis. We might well ask in which of [these] projects the spirit of God is most surely at work!" [5]

Or consider the general perspective of WASPs when they attempt to deal with problems of youth or delinquency. The *family* is usually regarded as the place for the ultimate cure of social and moral problems of our time. Any conversation about juvenile delinquency concludes, ultimately, with the truism that the home is the answer. We point with concern to the breakdown in family life, to the absence of the family altar, and the need for families to spend more time together. Remember, "the family that prays together and plays together stays together." This is our motto, and it is a good motto. It is true and accurate to stress the importance of Christian family life. There is every reason for Christians to be concerned about its breakdown.

However, this preoccupation with the family as the ultimate solution to our Christian problems indicates one more time the nearly complete unfamiliarity of the WASPs with life in the other America. Michael Harrington exposes our naïveté clearly:

So it is that the adolescents roam the streets. For the young, there is no reason to stay around the house. The street is a moment of relief, relaxation, and excitement. The family, which should be a bulwark against the sheer

[5] *Ibid.*

physical misery of the poor, is overwhelmed by the environment.

In this context, some of the rhetorical pieties of this society take on an unwitting irony. For example, here is Mayor Wagner of New York discussing the role of the promiscuous, addicted, violent girls in the gang wars of his city: "Of course," he continued, "the ultimate prevention of delinquency must begin in the home. Nothing the Government of the community can do," he said, "will substitute for the reassertion of parental control."

The only trouble with this familiar formula is that delinquency begins in the home and that these girls are, in all probability, fleeing a domestic shambles. To wait around until parental authority reasserts itself under the present conditions is to wait forever.[6]

My wife and I learned something about the real nature of this problem when we took into our home an eighteen-year-old boy who came from a culturally deprived family. The boy's mother, a widow, "encouraged" her children to leave home when they reached age eighteen and no longer merited Social Security payments from the government. This fact, in and of itself, ought to have shown us that the boy's mother was something less than a candidate for woman of the year, but we faithfully adhered to our middle-class belief that the home is a solution to all problems. However, our experience in the months following was a genuine education in the facts of life. The first eighteen years of his life had been daily lessons in anx-

[6] *The Other America,* p. 133.

iety, survival, frustration, and hopelessness. The Christian home as an answer was no answer to Jim's condition, his attitude, and his daily dilemmas. Too much water had already flowed over the dam, or perhaps we should say through the prison of his experience.

Most ironic of all is the fact that the local church, when it *tries* to be interested in the problems of race relations, poverty, migrant labor, or discrimination of other kinds—in short, when it is interested in crossing over into the world of the have-nots—usually misses the point. Its approach to the problem primarily consists of two methods: simple charity and dandy resolutions. By simple charity we mean the various acts of doing good deeds in small ways for individuals or small groups of individuals who have troubles. A home burns down, and the congregation may collect money and goods for the victims. At Christmas people whose names are referred to the churches by the Salvation Army or its counterparts are "adopted" by church groups, and they are given gifts of food, clothing, and toys. There may be sewing groups who make or repair clothing which will help some of the needy in this country or abroad, and we have already mentioned the rummage sales, the income from which will help buy *new* robes for the choir. We sometimes remember that there is some "outreach" money in the church budget which somebody somewhere will eventually get to help somebody else somewhere else who is in need.

The other approach is participated in by local

churches but is primarily demonstrated at the denominational level—the making of noble resolutions. Sometimes the resolutions are specific and inspirational, and other times they are merely platitudes, favoring the brotherhood of man and opposing man's inhumanity to man. In recent years, too, there have been springing up in local churches—as well as in the service clubs, etc.—small clusters of individuals whom we might call "Larry Liberals." These are the persons who articulate their thoughts about problems at the national and international levels. They speak for mankind. They favor demonstrations in the South, if they live in the North, and may even stand for integrated neighborhoods in Detroit, if they live in Kalamazoo. They may have been outspoken in favor of civil rights bills, and they like the urban renewal program. They also support the liberal resolutions which the churches make, and they may work to get them worded as strongly as possible.

Both simple charity and high-minded resolutions are too little and too late, however. Simple charity is worth something, at times a great deal, to be sure; and in a day when even this much is conspicuous by its absence, we can be grateful for any acts of kindness, no matter how small. Admittedly, it is sometimes difficult even to get a resolution out of some church groups, and we cannot underestimate the dedication of many of the persons who have worked hard to get such public statements. Nevertheless, both these approaches fail to help WASPs break out of their ghetto of indifference. Simple charity, even when sincere and genuinely sympathetic rather than condescending, does not even scratch the surface of the gap between the haves and the have-nots. On the other hand, the resolutions which favor the great causes that ultimately *will* make a difference usually fail to generate much passion for the *people* who need help and understanding. They are impersonal and, by their very nature, general. Like Charlie Brown in the *Peanuts* comic strip, Larry Liberal often is for *mankind* but may not be able to stand the sight of *people*.

The only really effective weapon the local church has used with much success is its prophetic voice, and the prophetic voice has had to be self-directed most of the time. Indeed, of all the institutions which have been under attack for failure in civil rights and in poverty, none has taken more criticism than the local church. None has probably deserved it more. The local church is a sitting duck for the prophet. The difference between public preaching about the love of God and the love of neighbor and the public practice of this gospel is deep and wide. Many young and concerned persons have turned away from the local church because of its failure to be a witnessing community. They have willingly joined the Peace Corps and they have risked their lives to go to Mississippi to register voters, but they are not much interested in the local church. That the parish church has lost and is losing the concerned young adult is a serious problem and a symptom of our sickness in the realm of social witness.

One young minister, wrestling with the question of whether or not to leave the parish church, expressed the feelings of many concerned Christians, both within and without the local congregation, in the following personal letter:

In a complex and ever-changing world, evident human need is all about us. Ideally, the local congregation ought to be, at least, the base from which some attempt is made to minister to that need. But the energies of the local congregation are more typically exhausted on such irrelevancies as rummage sales, covered dish suppers, and petty in-fighting of the most exhausting and unproductive sort.

Here, in fact, is the real tragedy, succinctly stated. The local church ought to be the base from which some attempt is made to minister to human need. It ought to be the place where noble resolutions are put into action. It ought to be the place least involved in the bureaucracy of the denomination. It ought to be the place where general needs stated in terms of statistics and profiles become translated into flesh and blood, into the sound of hungry babies and anxious mothers, the place where frustrations are shared, and where heartfelt expressions of love are turned into action.

It ought to be all these things, but it is not. The have-nots lie bleeding along the road, and the haves are passing them by on their way to church. And because of our failures, the church is losing the very people who can help it the most—the concerned persons who want to break out of the ghetto of indifference.

This much is obvious. If the gap is bridged, the initiative will have to be taken by the white, Anglo-Saxon Protestants. A disturbing fact of life is simply that the present attitude in the typical WASP church will keep the residents of other America away in droves. To begin with, the have-nots would have to drive to the suburbs even to find middle-class Christians in their natural habitat, and this is not going to happen. There are, of course, many large and prominent downtown churches in our cities which stand now in or near a blossoming slum; but, with some significant exceptions, the strategy of these churches is to hire a powerful pulpit voice which will keep attracting the old members back into the city on Sunday from the suburbs to which they have escaped. Chances are that few of the members of these churches live nearby. Even if they did, however, the program as presently constituted in most WASP churches would be of little value to the have-nots who might, by coincidence, stumble into the building.

A few churches have faced this fact and taken advantage of their opportunities to minister to the neighborhoods where they are—a downtown slum, a Puerto Rican ghetto, or a rural area seasonally populated by migrant workers. The church of Jesus Christ, fortunately, is not exemplified only by its middle-class, lily-white congregations, but also by the East Harlem Protestant Parish, by inner-city work in Chicago and other large cities, and by individual congregations here and there who are living testimonies to the truth that in Christ there is no East nor West, black nor white, rich nor poor. Indeed, it is a serious mistake to think that Christianity is losing its vitality simply because of the failures of its individual WASP congregations. After all, the Negro churches in the South which have been burned to the ground and those courageous Christians who have spent their lives in service to God and people could very well be the norm for Christian witness, even though they represent the minority of church members in terms of numbers. The Christ of their faith is the same worshiped in name by many others. The difference is in the degree of commitment which those members demonstrate.

This book, however, is not primarily about them, partly because they are clearly exceptions and partly because we WASPs can—and frequently do—dismiss them as "special" cases, just as Albert Schweitzer was sometimes dismissed as a special kind of person who did not have the same needs and drives and attitudes as normal folks. Many of us have thrilled to the real-life stories of Christians who have gone to the scene of great poverty or trouble, there to make their witness. One can scarcely read *Come Out the Wilderness* or *God's Colony in Man's World* and not be tempted, as he reads, to think that he must leave the relative comfort of where he is and join those Christians on the front lines. We may even be tempted to leave the church altogether, and more than one conscientious social worker, college teacher, civil rights enthusiast, or pastor has done just that. Because the witness in behalf of the have-nots by the haves has been so pathetically insignificant, we ought not be surprised that conscientious persons desert the local church, often sadly, because they feel it is an irrelevant and outmoded structure.

Yet it is in the local church where our real crisis exists. With all its faults and with all its failures, the persons within the established churches still constitute the groups with the best potential for helping the causes most important to the welfare of the have-nots. The power structure of an entire community may be represented in a given church on a given Sunday morning. Social workers may cut through eight miles of red tape and talk their way past a half-dozen staccato-speaking secretaries in order to reach a government official or a slum landlord when a concerned Christian or a sensitive pastor would be able to walk up to him after church and say, "Say, Harry, I'd like to talk to you a minute about. . . ."

That the church is populated by members who *could* change things for the better is self-evident. That they frequently are close-minded about their responsibilities and unwilling to share in the cause is also painfully obvious. However, that this is an impossible situation which cannot be changed and that there are impossible people who cannot be redeemed are not self-evident facts. Indeed, to say this is to dismiss the power of the gospel. God bless the man or woman who gives up on the local parish church because of his discouragement with it and his call to serve elsewhere; but God *help* those who stay with it for the *sake of both* the haves and the have-nots.

We must also see that the task of the church is not just to help the have-nots in whatever ways we can. It is also to face the fact that the WASPs live in their ghetto, and they, too, need help to escape from it. The irony of our situation is that the heart of the solution, ultimately, to the revolutions of our time in race relations, minority rights, and poverty is essentially a Christian one that must be faced at the local level. During the 1964 presidential election the point was made again and again that prejudice cannot be eliminated by coercion, that laws cannot make people take care of one another, and that morality cannot be legislated. These statements were ignored by most people because they seemed to be mere excuses for not doing anything, a process of rationalization which eased the consciences of the haves as they considered their relationship to the have-nots, about whom they knew little and with whom, on the personal level, they had very little contact.

Yet, these statements are true! That they became clichés cannot be denied, but the point is that the Christian church by its very thrust toward the hearts of men and by its very message of inward commitment is oriented toward changing the motives of mankind. Conversion is certainly not a strange word to the middle-class, Protestant church member, although frequently it has been used in too narrow a way. It has social implications, and the converted person ought to be understood as one who is changed in his attitude toward all men—even the have-nots—as well as in his relationship with God.

That the majority of our church members have not become aware of these implications is as much an indictment of the *worship* of the churches as it is the *witness* of the churches. Basically, the reasons why the separation has come about are not new. Selfishness, self-righteousness, greed—these are at the heart of the problems of society, and these have been the targets of the Christian gospel for two thousand years. There is a direct and distinct connection between the failures of the church as a community of worship and its failure to witness in the world. Nominalism is partly the cause of this failure; token participation leads to watered-down witness. The absence of personal disciplines of prayer and Bible study is part of the reason why slums exist, even though the connection is far from obvious. The local church is fighting a war on several fronts, or ought to be, at the same time. Whether it is winning or losing is an open question, but it is all part of the same war.

Finally, the church has some powerful allies, if it but knew it. More accurately, we might say it needs to accept some strange bedfellows in the name of Christ. Concerned Christians, at least, are often inclined to think that the church is not present or involved unless the local congregation is specifically present, identifiable, and preferably led by a reverse-collared pastor and six acolytes swinging incense pots. The social action committee is expected to "do something," and when it does nothing, many Christians assume nothing is being done. Contemporary theology has been de-emphasizing the differences between the sacred and the secular, but in the minds of most Protestants, the church is not present unless you can see its official seal and touch the hem of the garments of its clergy. **1388571**

Our tragedy would not be so great, in other words, if the church did not try to compete with other agencies for time and personnel, at least in the realm of social witness. Nor would our problem be so great if churches at the local level would take the ecumenical movement seriously and pool their own meager resources. The church has not failed so miserably if we think of it, properly, as the people of God who are scattered and working in the world. Then, instead of wringing our hands when a man chooses social work instead of the pastoral ministry, we could clap them for joy. Some of the huge social problems of our day require specialists and carefully trained social technicians, psychologists, slum clearance experts, teachers, and counselors. There needs to be a valid call to these vocations *in the name of the church,* and the whole definition of Christian vocation needs desperately to be broadened.

The feebleness of the local church is not necessarily indicated by a young person's choosing social work over the pastoral ministry, although when relatively few choose formal church work—as is the case now—it should make us take stock of our ministry. The irrelevance of the local church is seen more clearly when it does not inspire its people to choose the several service vocations or, equally important, does not inspire its members in "regular" vocations to interpret their roles as opportunities for public witness and concern for the have-nots. Our total problem is a shortage of persons concerned about the anxieties and needs of people on the other side of the tracks, the people of other races, or the invisible residents of other America. The church of Jesus Christ is at its best when it is identified by the commitment of its people, rather than by its official insignias and special symbols.

Paradoxically, at a time when the local church is under more attack and receiving (deservedly so!) more criticism than ever before in its history, there is more hope for it than there has been in a long time. Many worried Christians within the churches have come to see the degree of hypocrisy, irrelevance, and rejection of its Lord which has been a plague on all our houses of worship. Those persons—both clergy and laity—who think that everything is really dandy because their churches added a Christian education wing last year or bought new curtains for the church kitchen last month have their heads in the sand on which their churches are built. However, the paradox is that we can have hope that the haves may someday bridge the gap which separates them from the have-nots simply because some Christians have awakened to the realization of how deep and how wide the chasm is that divides the two worlds. A few have, after many years, discovered that we have a problem.

To have the hope and the faith that local groups of Christian people can rise above the social and economic boundaries of life that define our respective ghettos is possibly naïve, maybe even absurd by this time. Already thousands of concerned persons have decided that the task is wholly one for government agencies and the church is little more than a cheering section at best and a bastion of conservative opposition at worst. There are many who have concluded that the chasm right now is too deep and too wide. Nevertheless, it must be bridged or at least some Christians must themselves be able to bridge it, or the local church will gradually become a provincial body of Christ, made of flesh without blood, of mind without heart.

As individuals or as groups, we may fail. It may be too late. The local church may necessarily have to change its present structure to such an extent that it (at least the church that is genuinely concerned about the have-nots) will be totally different from the church we now see before us.

In the meantime, however, we need to remember that the chasm is not the only thing which is deep and wide. Those who remember old camp songs will recall that there is something else "deep and wide"—the love and forgiveness of God for all men who seek him, even the WASPs confined to their ghettos of indifference.

THE PHARISEES AND
THE REPUBLICANS

2

On one occasion the author was a visiting minister in a large city and in the process of a sermon used an illustration about the exploitation of the poor by slum landlords. The illustration had to do with the fact that slum property, especially in large metropolitan areas, is usually not owned by evil and greasy men who have a working relationship with the Mafia or who sit in plush offices someplace, rubbing their hands together greedily at the very thought of next month's rent. Instead, it was pointed out, slum property is often owned by large, respectable businesses, such as insurance companies, or by friendly, amiable WASPs who simply do not see the connection between their church lives and their business lives.

Immediately after the sermon the resident pastor told me that I had, unknowingly and accidentally, described one member of his congregation almost perfectly. He said that this particular man could not have been more perfectly identified if he had been asked to stand and wave to the congregation. About that time I looked up to see this very man walking toward me, which presented the possibility that we were about to have a genuine confrontation between prophet and sinner.

The confrontation never took place. Instead of anger or remorse or defensiveness, the man clasped my hand, thanked me for the sermon, and asked me if I would be interested in coming to that church as their full-time pastor, since the present minister was leaving soon. My "prophetic" sermon had made *no* impact on that man, at least any that could be observed. I might as well have said nothing. Afterward, the resident pastor and I discussed this event and tried to analyze how such seeming indifference could be possible. His comment was straight to the point: "Well, ol' Fred probably just regarded what you said as so much preacher-talk and nothing to take seriously."

For better or worse, his analysis is probably right. Much of the "prophetic" witness which comes from the pulpit is totally discounted simply because it is "preacher-talk." Preachers are *supposed* to be against sin in general or even, occasionally, in particular. However, they are seldom taken seriously because it is more or less their job to speak out against naughtiness and stuff. Most of them don't drink, so they can preach against drinking. Few of them own much property, therefore the property owner discounts what the minister says about slum investments. Most ministers are too poor to gamble, therefore it is regarded as their job to oppose legalized gambling. After all, if there were no sins such as these, what *would* the poor fellows talk about anyhow?

Unfortunately, the process we have here caricatured is more often the case than not. The ability of the human mind to rationalize behavior is only compounded when a person is in church. Like David in the Old Testament, we seldom get the message until a finger is pointed at us and a voice says, "Thou art the man!" Even then we are inclined to think that some mistake has been made, and everything will seem better in the morning after a good night's sleep.

Yet, here is the beginning of the problem of the haves and their indifference toward the have-nots. Before the gap between them can be bridged, before the causes of the have-nots will be championed by the Christian churches with any degree of commitment, before any genuine motivation for WASPs to break out of their ghetto of indifference can be felt, we will have to have a confrontation with ourselves and with our fellow church members. Somehow, in some way, the process of rationalization which has protected the white, Anglo-Saxon Christian from his responsibility toward his invisible neighbors must be broken down. As we suggested earlier, the churches ought to be the best equipped agencies in the world to deal with sin, and the business of prejudice, of exploitation, or of calculated indifference is the church's business. It must be dealt with before any genuine concern for neighbor will rise up in the hearts and minds of people in local churches.

There was a time, of course, when the primary approach of the churches to all problems of sin was relatively simple. All that was necessary, it was felt, was to convert the individual and, once this was done, it was assumed he was ready to live the ethical life and see his duty to his neighbors. To some extent this approach was effective in increasing an individual's ability to change some of his habits, and many a man gained the will to give up drinking or playing the horses or beating his wife. Often, however, there seemed to be some question as to whether or not *genuine* conversion had taken place. Furthermore, one's duty toward his neighbor was not always self-evident. When the social gospel was popular, the church for awhile worked hard to confront particular ethical and moral problems, and the shotgun approach became less popular. Thousands of Christians became convinced that war, illiteracy, disease, and poverty were going to be eliminated in their generation, and when they did not disappear, it was a discouragement to many a concerned Christian.

Both these approaches failed, as Reinhold Niebuhr and others showed us, because they did not take seriously the connection between the sinfulness of the spirit and the social responsibility of men. Not only do we fight for the causes of the have-nots on the field of battle —in settlement houses, civil rights demonstrations, industrial missions, or at city hall—we also function as part of the war effort on the home front by getting men to enlist. We have been telling people that somebody *ought* to care more for his neighbors or that somebody exploits his neighbor, but we have had trouble in getting the WASPs to see that "somebody" is good old number one.

The reason for this is the fact that sinfulness, as does disease, takes many forms, wears many faces, and frequently builds up tremendous resistance to the usual and familiar cures. We who are white, middle-class, and Protestant have been cultivating a special form of sinfulness for years and have refined it into an art form of self-rationalization. Before any bridges can be built to the world of the have-nots, we will have to become aware of the *need* to get to the other side. We will have to see our problem before we will have incentive to deal with it.

Most of the time the special sinfulness of the haves takes two forms, closely related to each other but with certain subtle differences. One form has had a name for a long time and was initially classified by Jesus in the New Testament: Pharisaism. Essentially, WASP Pharisaism is a form of self-justification by faith. It has several different components, but all have the common bond of being attitudes that are retroactive: They justify what one does or wants to believe *after the fact*. Conversely, it is implied, if the have-nots would just do or behave as they, the haves, have done and behaved, their situation would not be so miserable.

For example, Pharisaism (or WASPism, if you prefer) is a dominant theme of the running commentary which bubbles forth whenever two or three are gathered together and end up discussing the welfare program. Douglas Cater, a Presbyterian minister who for several years has been a caseworker with the Cook County department of public aid in Chicago, is familiar with this attitude, and his recognition of it is implied throughout an article which appeared last year in *The Christian Century*. Mr. Cater paraphrases the attitude by putting it in a biblical context:

"Depart from me, . . . into the eternal fire . . . for I was hungry and you gave me no food, . . . naked and you did not clothe me. . . ."

"But, Lord, what kind of talk is this? We didn't really let you go hungry; we gave you $23 a month for food, plus $5 a month for clothing, to say nothing of $9 for personal incidentals and $3 for laundry! We admit you couldn't live very well on it, but we didn't let you starve! We even paid your doctor bills. We kept you alive. What kind of ingrate are you? After all, if you wanted more you should have gone out and earned it!" [1]

WASPism is obvious in the statements, heard so often, that welfare recipients are primarily a bunch of "chislers" who could support themselves if they wanted to do so. Read the letters to the editor column on a regular basis and you will find many which compare the good guys (the respectable, tax-paying citizen) with

[1] "The Church and the 'Reliefers,'" p. 232. Copyright 1965 by Christian Century Foundation. Reprinted by permission from the February 24, 1965 issue of *The Christian Century*.

the bad guys (the social parasites) who live off the blood and sweat of the hard-working minority.

The letters to the editor column, as a matter of fact, is a gold mine of such rationalizations. A random collection of some of the relevant comments is more than just a little revealing:

My business is seasonal but when I need workers I have to hire college kids because the lazy bums on relief are just that—lazy bums.

Most Negroes in this city, I am sure, heartily disapprove of the demonstrations in Selma.

There has always been work and there will always be work for any person with initative. . . . A few good kicks in you-know-where would help cut the cost of welfare in half.

I, for one, am tired of subsidizing the birth of illegitimate children [through the Aid to Dependent Children program].

If the do-gooders and bleeding hearts would just stay home and mind their own business there would be no occasion for police brutality.

Some of them [the reliefers] wouldn't be in such bad shape if they didn't spend so much of their handout on booze.

How completely these statements summarize the attitude of the WASPs is difficult to say, but certainly they are not unusual. The key to a faith by self-justification is the psychological ability to compare one's self to the lot of the have-nots and then make the assumption that it is, somehow, their own fault, or to convince one's self that they are not really as bad off as the "bleeding hearts" would have us think.

A community education consultant for the national Small Business Administration—a WASP organization if ever one existed—presented a similar view in a public speech. The news account of this speech included a tirade against "laziness." "They call it a war on poverty. What they *really* need is a war on laziness. I'm getting sick and tired of paying to help support some eight million people who are too damned lazy to do something for themselves." Commenting on this nation's moral decay, the speaker called the welfare and relief programs "the greatest illegitimacy incentive program ever known," pointing out that the state of New York's relief load is "10 times greater now than it was during the depression."

Much of the effort of the welfare department is based on this very philosophy (which is often echoed by state legislators). It usually runs something like this: "Give the reliefers as little money as possible, just barely enough to keep them from starving, thereby making them so uncomfortable that they will bend their energies to finding other sources of income and will get off the taxpayer's back." Similar to the Pharisee of old the WASP says: "I thank God I am not like that tax receiver over there who lives off my income."

We see the attitude articulated, too, in the resentment exhibited by many middle-class people against the ADC mother who has illegitimate children. Douglas Cater analyzes it in this way:

> A.D.C. women are thought to be not only cheating the taxpayers but enjoying themselves sexually in the process. They are seen as having no restraint, no inhibition and no sense of responsibility, asking moreover to be supported by those who restrain themselves from such licentiousness. One detects a note of intense jealousy underlying this surface resentment.
>
> The problem is more than mere jealousy, however; there is tremendous confusion about the whole area of sexual standards. The "respectable" middle class person is greatly perplexed as to what he believes (or thinks he should believe) concerning sex. Much is being written about increased premarital sexual relationships on college campuses and about increased adultery in suburbia. The middle class Christian is not sure where he should stand on these matters, and he is infuriated by people who seemingly are untroubled about them and who simply enjoy themselves "doing what comes naturally." Consonant with these feelings, he is likely to be opposed to free birth control services for A.D.C. mothers on the grounds that this would allow sexual license without any "retribution" whatever.[2]

The southern WASP, who has many northern counterparts, has comforted himself for years with the belief that the Negro's lot is just the way he wants it. We project our own feelings, or the way we hope he feels, on to the Negro-in-general, and this, again, enables us to escape any moral responsibility for getting in-

Ibid., p. 234.

volved in his life. They, and often the poor whites as well, are said to be "happier than we are," living the carefree life, free from responsibility and cares. As one hard-working Protestant put it when speaking to his son about a certain poor family: "They are happier than we are, son. They don't have to worry about the high taxes or the stock market or any of the rest of it." The intellectual may look at a run-down mountain house, as he drives through the Appalachians in the summer, and think of Rousseau's "natural man," eventually deciding that those people are fortunate to be exempt from the strains and tensions of the middle class.

So ends the lesson on one of the special forms of sinfulness which is the burden of the haves. The human mind can send rockets to the moon, but it can also convince us that the poor are not really poor, the hungry really have enough to eat, the person dressed in rags likes his clothes to have plenty of ventilation, and slum-dwelling mothers have babies just for the fun of it. Thinking such as this is very effective in keeping both the haves and the have-nots in their respective ghettos.

The other form of sinfulness which we demonstrate over and over again is similar to the Pharisaism we have just described but with a different emphasis. Whereas we may try to convince ourselves that the other Americans are not really so badly off, we also are able to convince ourselves that we are relatively successful in life due to our resourcefulness, integrity, and personal achievements. Mainly for the sake of a catchy title for this chapter, we have called this form of sinfulness "Republicanism." Certainly it is not limited to Republicans, but the vice of which we speak is a corruption of one of the virtues normally associated with the party of rugged individualism: self-reliance. Self-reliance is a virtue, but it is also, for the Christian, a positive handicap in his efforts to escape from his ghetto.

This is a virtue which has made our country great, and many of us view with alarm the growing tendency of our citizenry to expect government to solve all our problems for us. Indeed, it is the partial theme of this book that the WASPS ought to get out of their ghetto and take care of their neighbors, wherever they may live. In this sense self-reliance continues to be a virtue if we consider it to be the effort by local people to solve their local problems. However, the corruption of this virtue is part of our problem, and we must face it squarely.

We have protected ourselves from the have-nots by substituting self-reliance (often a private myth) for sympathy. Nearly every teenager is familiar with this philosophy because he has heard his father tell him, when he sought to borrow the car, "When I was your age I had to walk five miles to school." Just as that teenager may begin to wonder if every parent of that generation lived five miles from school, so does this cry of self-credit begin to have a tone of sounding brass and a nostalgic symbol. In brief, this attitude says, "We did it; why can't they?"

There was a time, of course, and not really many years ago, when our society could not have been called affluent, in the sense in which it is so described today. Either we or our parents may very well have come from humble circumstances and, by hard work, made good. Just as many persons are trying to work their way into heaven by good deeds and righteous living, so many have come to justify—probably subconsciously—the gap between the haves and the have-nots on the grounds that they worked and pulled themselves up by their bootstraps and so ought others.

The trouble with this rather comforting belief, the factor which makes it a subtle form of sinfulness, is that it fails to give credit to God and others who make it possible for us to be so "self-reliant." We see it especially evident at Thanksgiving, a time when Americans are supposed to be giving thanks to God for his mercies but which instead has come to be an orgy of self-congratulation. "See how well we feed our families! We did it all with our own little hatchets." One would almost get the impression that we had grown the wheat, made the bread, and invented the internal combustion engine which was in the truck that hauled the loaves to the store. The Pharisees and the "Republicans" have much in common: a problem in modern self-righteousness.

The way in which this attitude helps widen the gap or at least keep the bridge from being built can best be seen in the lack of sensitivity to the stultifying effects of the have-not environment. We are inclined to take credit for our achievements and blame the have-nots for their failures. This might be a reasonable claim *if* more of us had been adopted, rather than born and nurtured by our real parents. Then, at least, we could have taken credit for our personal attractiveness or winning ways that would have inspired someone to adopt us for his own. However, most of us were not adopted, and we are the way we are and we have achieved much of what we have achieved because parents gave us a helping hand, on the shoulder or elsewhere, or maybe loaned us money, or because we inherited a certain amount of I.Q., or because we were exposed to certain cultural advantages that are virtually unknown to the have-nots.

In short, we WASPs have little reason even to take credit for our own initiative, which we are inclined to glorify. True, no person is ever completely a victim or a product of his environment, and there are many who have worked their way out of a slum or out from under the burden of being a Negro in white America. Nevertheless, these persons are the exceptions, not the rule, and most of the time the man who wins the race is going to be the fellow who does not have to carry a fifty-pound weight on his back. The poor breed children who will, themselves, more than likely be poor. Being a Negro, even in our so-called "Great Society," is still a liability. The migrants who roam the countryside seldom have any political or social or educational helping hand. We, primarily by the grace of God, are not wearing their shoes. It is not, as we might like to believe, the natural result of our own initiative or our own goodness.

We who are the Pharisees will have to be confronted with our own special sinfulness. Our attitudes will necessarily have to change. Not only will we fail to get involved in public and private ways in the life and trials of the invisible Americans, but we will fail even to regard their plight with sympathy and understanding. It is, after all, asking a great deal for persons voluntarily to join a sit-in or demonstration or to identify with the children of the slums by living there. Our problem is even deeper, though, for by our inability to see our own self-righteousness, we may refuse to support the efforts of *other* individuals or even the government to help the have-nots.

So, we in the middle-class churches often become the bastion of middle-class morality, a stronghold of thousands of decent, moral, basically kind, and usually sensitive people who make no connection between private beliefs and public responsibilities. We may voluntarily rebuild a neighbor's barn which has burned but oppose adequate public assistance programs to raise the level of family life in the slums. We turn away from the suggestion of an adequate minimum wage "because some jobs are not worth even a dollar an hour." We discriminate in employment "because we have an obligation to the stockholders, and we can't take risks in the business." We seldom seek, nor get, quality education in deprived neighborhoods, yet we oppose with passion the bussing of Negro children into better school districts. The retirement homes our churches build often cost much more than our needy aged can afford, and we fail to subsidize these homes because we need our denominational capital to build new churches in the suburbs. As Martin Luther King has said, the church is "often the taillight instead of the headlight" in the battle against discrimination.

Yes, in both large government and denominational programs to help the have-nots there is bureaucracy. Yes, indeed, there is waste and there are some chislers on the relief roles and there are some lazy people who think the world owes them a living. The process of rationalization in which we persist is possible because there is some truth in it, and because we can usually illustrate what we want to believe with an unfortunate personal example. Mainly, however, it is possible because we simply wish it to be true. Fundamentally, for the Christian, it is not possible to justify our indifference in this way. We do not help or seek to help persons because they *deserve* it or because they are *"our kind"* but only because they are children of God.

Since our sinfulness is special and subtle, we must confront it in ways other than the traditional ones. For too many years local churches have selected the sins they are going to oppose with care, and they have carefully avoided getting involved in the sin of self-righteousness in any specific way. We have concentrated on the kind of personal vices illustrated in a little jingle that many midwestern fans have heard as part of the cheers at athletic contests:

> We don't smoke and we don't chew,
> And we don't go with girls that do!
> We're going to win this ball game!

The connection between winning ball games and the personal habits of the cheerleaders may not be self-evident, but the jingle does illustrate the pride that often comes from choosing some sins while rejecting others. Most WASPs don't smoke or chew or go with girls that do, or, if they do, they don't worry about it very much. The point is that we must see, as we have failed to see, the social, as well as the personal, nature of sin.

To break through the self-righteousness of modern Pharisaism, we will have to be more direct in our public and private devotions. For example, the general confession has been standard equipment in many Protestant churches for years, yet not many members are thinking of themselves as "sheep who have gone astray." The general confession may be too general. What we need is to supplement it with a particular confession.

By this we mean that it is a Christian responsibility to learn the facts about ourselves and the nature of poverty, discrimination, and the world of the have-nots. We should sponsor study courses in the welfare program as we do in foreign missions. Douglas Cater suggests several topics which ought to be taken seriously and, we might add, be understood as part of the church's task of confronting its people with their sinfulness.[3]

1. *Common accusations made against welfare recipients.* "These should be examined in detail and truth should be distinguished from mere rumor." Cater emphasizes that "cheating," while really a very small problem in light of the total amount of money and persons involved, is sometimes "the *only* way in which a recipient can attain a reasonably 'decent' standard of living, since the avenues to this end which are open to the middle class person are simply unavailable to most reliefers."

2. *The social conditions which cause the welfare rolls to swell.* Christians should study the cause of unemployment in their own communities. Then there is the whole problem of housing, including the problem of the ghetto as well as our own middle-class fears of open occupancy.

3. *The problem of birth control services.* It would be a genuine religious quest if we took the time and the energy to understand the mores and unstable social milieu of lower-class Negroes and whites. Study books, such as *One-Fifth of the Nation* by Elma L. Greenwood and *Who Cares?* by Janet Harrington and Muriel

[3] *Ibid.,* p. 235.

Webb, ought to be regarded both as tools for study and devotional contemplation.

It would be a good idea, too, for adult groups in local churches to make the rounds with one of the social workers in the welfare department, seeing with their own eyes some of the "chislers" about whom they complain. This was done by at least one church group, and it was like a divine revelation to some of the participants. Instead of a bunch of drunks sleeping one off, they found aged and blind people, elderly men who cut their own wood and hauled water from a pump to wash by, and deserted mothers trying to care for several small children while lacking both money and knowledge in how to do so. Or it might be a religious pilgrimage for Christian groups to contact their local mental health office sometime and see how frequently mentally disturbed people are held in jail and, furthermore, how many of the ones who are held in jail are both poor and retarded. The point is that it is a matter of Christian responsibility, a matter of public devotion and confession, that the WASPs leave their beaten paths and confront the truth, the truth about the other Americans and, equally important, the truth about their own rationalizations.

In addition to this confrontation with the facts, we are going to have to create some new worship forms and methods which will help twentieth-century people face twentieth-century sinfulness in a relevant way.

Most of us do not make a mental connection with the poverty-stricken when we consider, in church, the need to love our neighbors. Fortunately, help is on the way. Concerned Christians are producing literature and liturgy which verbally, at least, confront us with the sins of today. One such work is a little book of prayers for "the natural man" by David Head which uses humor and irony to make its point. Included in this work are both genuine devotional experiences as well as satirical "prayers" which would be prayed if we would express our true and honest feelings. For example, David Head suggests this "litany" to help us when we pray:

We miserable owners of increasingly luxurious cars, and ever-expanding television screens, do most humbly pray for that two-thirds of the world's population which is under-nourished;
You can do all things, O God.

We who seek to maintain a shaky civilization do pray most earnestly that the countries which suffer exploitation may not be angry with the exploiters, that the hungry may not harbour resentment against those who have food, that the down-trodden may take it patiently, that nations with empty larders may prefer starvation to communism, that the "have-not" countries may rejoice in the prosperity of those that have, and that all people who have been deeply insulted and despised may have short memories;
You can do all things, O God.

We who prosper through the work and patience of
others pray that we may have the sense not to
drive them too far;
  You can do all things, O God. . . .

That the sick may be visited, the prisoner cared
for, the refugee rehabilitated, the naked clothed,
the orphan housed, and that we may be allowed to
enjoy our own firesides, evening by evening, in
peace;
  You can do all things, O God.

O Son of God, we beg, we beseech, we supplicate,
we petition, we implore You to hear us.
  Lord, be good to us.
  Christ, make things easy for us.
  Lord, deliver us from the necessity of doing anything.[4]

The National Council of Churches has been working
in this area, as it recognizes the need for more explicit
devotional material. Last spring, for example, Christian
women all over America used a worship service which
combined scriptural passages and the facts of life about
poverty in America. It included statistics about poverty,
moving poetry, and a specific call to specific action:

Who will work for more adequate public assistance
  programs to raise the level of family life and restore hope?
Who will work for a higher minimum wage?

[4] *He Sent Leanness* (New York: The Macmillan Company, 1959),
pp. 23-24.

Who will work to eliminate discrimination in employment?

The fact that even this worship service undoubtedly fell on some deaf ears is beside the point. Jesus Christ did not reach everyone, and he had the most difficulty in reaching the Pharisees. Nevertheless, when our rationalizations are confronted in the context of worship, we are moving in the right direction.

The WASPs are in a position analagous to that of the alcoholic. Persons experienced in Alcoholics Anonymous and in formal psychiatric care of alcoholics know that little can be done to help them until they are able to recognize the need within themselves for help. They often have to reach their "low bottom," that point in their lives when conditions of health or mental stability are so horrible that they will gain the desire to quit drinking. Those of us who socially and economically live and move in the world as white middle-class Protestants have, first of all, to find the point in our lives when concern for the have-nots can no longer be avoided by our rationalizations and self-deceptions. The fact is, you see, that all we like sheep *have* gone astray and we *have* left undone the things we ought to have done, among them being the avoidance of love and responsibility for the poor, the aged, the forgotten, the hopeless, and the ignorant. Felicia Komia says,

The truth is that our civilisation is *not* Christian;
It is a tragic compound of great ideals and fearful practice,

Of high assurance and desperate anxiety,
Of loving charity and fearful clutching of possessions.[5]

In our day, in this time and this place, Christians are going to have to rise above their preoccupation with simple personal morality by going deeper within themselves to see the sinfulness of their social irresponsibility. Until we lose the blindness of our rationalizations, we will be unable to see our brothers lying along the road.

I pass you by like a hundred others
who also pass you by—
and the road may be the road
from Jerusalem to Jericho for all we know.
I would like to put my hand on your shoulder
and say to you, "Comrade,
there is One who died for us
and dying made us blood brothers."
But I am filled with the cowardice of the well-dressed—
for clothes are by no means flimsy
when it comes to erecting barriers
between man and man.
I am afraid you will wake with a start
and betray resentment in your eyes
as you see in me what I really am—
your well-dressed enemy.
And then you will acknowledge defeat
and put on your mask of patient stupidity.
You will jump up and dust the seat

[5] *Cry, The Beloved Country* (New York: Friendship Press, 1955), p. 38.

and grin and point to it with a flourish of your hand.
You will want us to sell our brotherhood
for eight *annas*.

Day after day I pass you by,
you the man by the roadside
and I the priest and the Levite rolled in one,
passing you by.[6]

[6] Chandran Devanesen, *The Cross Is Lifted* (New York: Friendship Press, 1954), pp. 47-48.

The local church, when it is preaching and teaching the gospel of Jesus Christ, is faced with a difficult dilemma. The matters about which its members usually get excited are seldom the things which do the most to further the kingdom of God on earth. We use the term "excited" in this instance advisedly, not casually, for sometimes church members do get "excited" (i.e., angry, indignant, confused, worried, etc.) over an important matter, such as during the integration of a church or when struck by a tornado or when the minister runs off with the church secretary. While most WASP church members are somewhat sophisticated and do not easily become emotionally involved in causes, major catastrophes usually catch their attention. There are some conscientious Christians, however, who feel that a major catastrophe is necessary before healthy excitement will be generated, but they may have become prematurely cynical. On the other hand, they may merely be ministers which, you will recall, means that pessimism about the world and about the church is a kind of occupational stance.

In the normal run of events, however, Protestant

churches are prone to get excited only over those matters which are relatively unimportant, such as building new additions, buying a new organ, putting on a dandy Christmas program, or inventing new gimmicks to get people "out" to a meeting. For all practical purposes, however, we care very little about whether the local Negro children get served root beer at a drug store, or whether the poor whites on the other side of town can read and write. Both local and international missionary work in our parishes has been, by and large, relegated to the afternoon amusement of conscientious women, and the local church which cares very much about its denomination's program in Hong Kong or on main street is unusual. The social action committee, or whatever it is called, is usually regarded as the Siberia of the committee structure, the really important responsibilities being carried by the trustees, the pastoral relations committee, or possibly the Christian education committee.

Such is the case, once again, because of the ghetto in which WASPs live. Ministers who may or may not have escaped the ghetto themselves may or may not be concerned about this fact, but it is a crucial fact of life that the WASP churches as groups and middle-class Christians as individuals are not excited over the invisible Americans. Yet, to put it bluntly, they had better become excited (i.e., involved, interested, concerned) or an entire younger generation is going to cross the local church off its list as irrelevant, immaterial, and uninteresting. Unless the local church can become, once again, neighbor-centered rather than building or program-centered, we are going to find ourselves sitting one day in the middle of our modernistically designed Protestant cathedrals wondering why we are there. We will be all dressed up with nothing to say.

Our problem is that we can scarcely get excited over problems we do not experience ourselves or the plight of people about whose circumstances we know very little. Even when we see that their plight is genuinely serious and even when we are able to recognize our own sinfulness of rationalization, our concern is still academic. We continue to have a hard time getting excited about the have-nots or their causes. We may preach at one another about it. We can even participate in the favorite indoor sport of the sociologists and the denominational executives, namely, of telling one another how ashamed we ought to be for discriminating against Negroes, neglecting the poor, and rejecting the migrant. The irony of the whole situation is that practically every Protestant church member who attends services with some degree of regularity knows that he *ought* to love his neighbor more.

His preacher has told him that he *ought* to love his neighbor. He is vaguely aware that the Bible says somewhere that we ought to care for one another. In his moments of compassion he may even wish he knew a few neighbors he could help. Poor Joe, the WASP, is in a dilemma similar to that pictured in a cartoon which showed a recent college graduate standing with his family immediately after the commencement exercises had concluded. The cartoon showed him standing in his cap and gown, clutching his diploma in his hand, and listening with anxiety on his face as his father says to him, "Well, son, don't just stand there. Start supporting yourself!" Our church members hear the command, "Don't just stand there. Start loving your neighbor!" and he, too, feels anxious or maybe even a little bit guilty.

Love and concern for neighbor cannot be programmed or commanded. What we in our churches can do is provide opportunity for Christian love to be experienced. Dorothy Hutchinson, a Quaker writer whose very life has been one of discipleship, has given an insight into how this might be possible. She has used the phrase "imaginative identification" as a synonym for love, and this phrase has some extremely important implications. It means to put yourself in another's place. It means to share his feelings. It means to get inside his skin, or, as another old saying has expressed it, to walk a mile in his moccasins. Should we provide one another with opportunities of imaginative identification, we might discover that spontaneous compassion can still be generated in the hearts and minds of the good-natured but indifferent "haves" of our churches.

The traditional approach to social action is the "preach-at-them" method. "You ought" or "you must" or you "really should" love your neighbor. It fails, usually, because it starts from a principle instead of a person. Or, at least, it fails to start from the right Christian principle that people are more important than the law. If the have-nots can become real flesh-and-blood people in our hearts and minds, then we may become concerned for them and about them, and we may be able to rise above our indifference to the preaching that tries to make us do something we do not feel.

See, for example, what happens frequently in the world. When an individual *personally experiences* a deep relationship or a crisis situation, he generalizes, often, his feelings into a principle. It may be the man whose wife is alive because of open-heart surgery. When the time comes for the heart fund drive, he is ready and willing to become involved. He has been there, and the principle that heart research is important is self-evident because personal experience demonstrates it to be true. A young college student may become an active civil rights demonstrator. Why? No, dear WASPs, there is little chance that he has become a victim of the communist conspiracy. More than likely the reason is —the motivating force is—that he has become a friend to a Negro, and it causes his juices to be stirred up when he realizes that in the land of the free and home of the brave a Negro citizen can't get his hair cut in his own hometown. The degradation which the friend experiences is taken on, vicariously, by the white student. He, in this way, *experiences* injustice. The task of the church and its individual members is to provide occasions for imaginative identification.

One such opportunity for this to happen is so simple and obvious that it is usually overlooked. We refer to the simple fact of friendship, of personal contact, or of inviting the people from the other ghetto into our own. In our own community several years ago, some persons invited a few others to a discussion group with refreshments. Included were some Negro acquaintances. The group continued meeting and grew. Now there are three large interracial, interfaith groups meeting regularly, and what is most important is that fact that many close and intimate friendships have been made among the group members. The white members of the group do not now have to be convinced that they "ought" to do something-or-other for the Negroes. Now it is at least as normal to want to be a part of their cause as it is to be the part of any other cause that would involve their white neighbors.

True, this particular effort was possible because of some personal friendships already in existence. It is also true that the Negroes involved are persons with whom it has been easy to make friends because they share many common social and cultural interests. Friendship cannot be forced, any more than marital love can be demanded by an irate husband. Nevertheless, this small effort illustrates one more facet of the reality of the WASP ghetto, in that many happy and wholesome friendships have been denied persons, white and black, because of the walls between them in a local community. Furthermore, it is sound sociological theory that out of artificial contacts genuine relationships frequently develop.

Another way in which imaginative identification can occur is seen in the practice that a few concerned individuals have followed. The welfare boards of a local community are usually in desperate need of persons who can house children who may be in the process of being placed in a permanent home. If Christians would, in fact, open their homes to a child or youth as a permanent residence, they would quickly break down all kinds of barriers that exist between the haves and the have-nots. Again, it is another testimony to our WASP provincialism that we are unaware of how many children are in need of a place to live and grow. Naturally, circumstances often dictate whether or not individual families can add another member to it on a permanent basis.

However, on a temporary or weekend basis, this is an opportunity to put faith into action. There is nothing very glamorous about taking a twelve-year-old boy or a nine-year-old girl into your home for a few days, especially when they come from homes that are scarcely fit for man or beast. Frequently, these children are not very lovable but instead are loaded with neurotic anxieties that can be spotted in the first five minutes.

Nevertheless, put yourself in the place of such a child; imaginatively identify, if you will. How would you feel if you were a child who had no place to go, no one to care, and no one who understands you? Forget for a moment that this is a product of an "evil" welfare system or that you have many inadequacies as a parent yourself. Think on the fact that here is a human being who is lonely, poor, and ashamed. How would you like to be treated if you were that child?

We are not speaking, please understand, of some breed of cat right out of *West Side Story* who has come to be a professional delinquent. We are speaking of poor, frightened children who need a large dose of interest and compassion. Yes, there are many dangers in doing this, and they must be recognized. Our own family experienced some of them when we opened our home to an eighteen-year-old boy who had been in trouble with the law, to which we referred earlier. Our mistake was that the boy, Jim, was a "project" in our minds, a "poor creature" we were going to help. Soon, we thought, he will be a model boy, and many white marks will be placed in the book of heaven by our name. We failed with Jim and in this adventure because we failed to be normal, natural, and understanding of this boy and his circumstances. We knew intellectually that he had a confused set of values and that his ways were foreign to ours, but we were unable to accept him in spite of these.

So there are dangers, real dangers, in doing this kind of thing. Yet, surely compassion and sympathy are not foreign to white, Anglo-Saxon Protestants. They may lie dormant, but the opening of one's home to a boy or girl may also open the doors of one's understanding. Indeed, the happy, well-adjusted home is one of the greatest resources which the haves can share with at least some of the have-nots. Churches, if they would, could rent or buy large houses and "staff" them with competent middle-aged people, if they could find such persons, and provide intermediate boarding homes for wards of the welfare department. Indeed, in many, many communities such a request has been spelled out in detail by local welfare boards. This would be church and state cooperating for the sake of people—in this case, lonely and frightened children. There are concerned Christians who sincerely want to help, but they have abdicated their opportunity to the professional social worker and welfare employee. The professionals often do a more personal and sympathetic job than many people assume, but basic, sincere feeling for children ought to be the stock-in-trade of middle-class Christians.

Some families, both Negro and white, have gone a second mile with this idea. In more than one community a few families collaborated in bringing from the large city slums several Negro children for a two-week vacation in rural or suburban America. Again, these families were not professional social workers; they were simply pleasant people who had fewer than the average number of prejudices. They were haves, without question. They were not involved in a crusade nor were they hoping to be martyrs. They simply hosted some children for awhile, let their own children play with them, took them camping or to the park, got angry with them when necessary, and learned more about some *bona fide* have-nots in two weeks than they had learned in their entire lives.

Surprisingly, the initial contact did not die a natural death. Nearly all the host families have kept in contact with "their children," one even having dropped in at their slum apartment to visit, and all remembering their children at Christmas and other holidays. It has not been a one-way street, either. The children and their families have answered the letters with their own. Certainly these return letters are different in their grammar and spelling, but the tone of genuine goodwill is characteristic of both parties. These particular haves probably would not choose these particular have-nots as regular traveling companions or bridge partners. To feel concern for invisible Americans is not forced friendship with persons with whom they have little in common socially and culturally. It does allow room, however, for a caring relationship to be established.

The ways in which the idea of imaginative identification can be developed are endless. One group of Christians worked with the warden of a state prison to enable some of his reforming prisoners (who are almost always have-nots) to go on tour and speak to school and church groups. This has proved to be an extremely effective way of breaking through a number of sociological stereotypes. Many of the young people who heard the "testimonies" of these prisoners suddenly found themselves thinking of them as human beings who were as much the victims of community and family indifference as they were responsible for their own crimes. They came to see that society and its individual members can be as calloused as any convict behind bars.

To gain real experience of life in hardship areas, thirty-nine DePauw students spent eight days in the field, going into selected economically blighted areas to see for themselves the conditions under which some persons live and work. Sponsored by the DePauw University Methodist Student Foundation, three groups visited and worked with, briefly, people in East Harlem slums, Brooklyn's depressed, crime-ridden Bedford-Stuyvesant area, and a big migrant camp near Hereford, Texas. The trips proved to be exercises in imaginative identification. One participant put it this way: "It's awfully easy to hole up in college, be a naïve and sheltered middle-class kid. . . . There is suffering—mental, physical, all kinds—in these places and we haven't experienced it. The best way to find out what it is like is to go there . . . get understanding and empathy with the problems and try to relate ourselves to it." The trips themselves were valuable for what deeds were accomplished, but more important was the effect they had on the *attitudes* of these students who will be WASP church members of tomorrow.

Visits to the nursing homes, to our mental hospitals,

to our prisons, to our homes for children, to our migrant camps, or to the various settlement houses in the slums are all good beginnings. We must hasten to note, however, that such visits are only a start, for it is amazing how we are able to see life in the raw and still rationalize ourselves out of feeling responsible. Going "slumming" is a far cry from imaginative identification.

Nevertheless, just seeing these segments of "other America" will be shocking to many of our provincial youth and adults. At least it will provide a new perspective and take them away from the scenic route which provides only picture postcard views of Appalachia or a Red Skelton understanding of the poor and the illiterate. In all the world there is still nothing quite so powerful for changing people in their thinking and attitudes as personal contact. Instead of chiselers, we may see children. Instead of Negroes to be feared or even pitied, one may find human beings who are persons of dignity and courage. Personal contact—especially when it is more than a brief, passing one—helps us build new stereotypes. Since the stereotypes we have now are usually distorted, there is every reason to believe that the new ones will be better and more accurate. There is even the possibility that we might discover beneath the dirt or the squalor a child of God. Before any discoveries can be made, however, we must begin the search.

There is also a form of "secondary" imaginative identification which helps break through barriers. Some denominations—with the Episcopal Church leading the way—are seeking to restore religious drama to the parish church scene. Not always do the plays which traveling church theater guilds perform deal with the themes of poverty or race relations, but more often than not they do. Often, too, the cast of players includes a Negro who may be spokesman for his race, and the expression of emotion which comes from a real, live person who has been there is sometimes a powerful means of identification by middle-class audiences.

Unfortunately, there is not really a large stock of Christian plays suitable for making this point. The Lord in all his wisdom and mercy has spared us from many Hollywood epics about religion that may have been conceived in the small minds of professional movie makers, but there have been enough produced to discourage persons from using religious drama in the church. How can one compete with the wide screen effect of *The Greatest Story Ever Told,* and who would want to do so? Unfortunately, the biblical epics often leave the viewer with only one reaction, "Gee, I wish Christ were around today to handle our problems." Seldom is one moved to deepen his relationship with his neighbor or inspired to make a concern for the have-nots a cause instead of an afterthought. It is a paradox, however, that one of the resources for imaginative identification which can be used is the secular drama. How strange it is that the movies and plays we call "religious" are often devoid of a genuine Christian theme, while there are "messages" at least in much secular drama.

The great advantage of secular drama is that it catches the viewer with his stereotypes down. WASPs wear many hats at different times during a week or even in a day. Whenever they attend a "Christian" meeting or gathering, they wear their "churchgoing" hat. They come with their defenses up and, like great sponges, are able to absorb any command to love their neighbor, any suggestion that they ought to change their ways, or any directive that they have a responsibility for the have-nots. As "churchgoers" WASPs seldom let their rationalizations and defenses down, and it is possible for them to ignore even good religious drama—whenever some appears.

However, when secular drama is used to show man's inhumanity to man or the power of compassion in *real* life, we are caught napping. We can imaginatively identify with it as a father, or friend, or simply a human being, and then there is hope for even a WASP heart to be strangely warmed. For example, one church group spent several weeks discussing various dramatic productions they saw on the television series *East Side, West Side*. (To call a television series "drama" may seem ludicrous to literary critics and purists, but perhaps we can be allowed this gesture if we recall that the series has since been taken off the air—one of the best indications of its merit.) Watching the weekly show was the class "homework," and it made a difference to some who watched it, especially when it was discussed in a Christian context.

One program in particular made an impact. Neil Brock, the main character who is a social worker in New York, appears on a TV panel to discuss with other fictional personalities the problems of the poor in the city. He is asked advice on one aspect of the problem, but he replies that one really ought to consult an expert on that question. He is told, in reply, that *he* is the "expert" because he is the social worker. To this Brock answered that the real "expert" is the baby who wakes in the middle of the night to see a rat crawling up the sheet toward his eyes. The "expert" is the mother who has to feed X number of children on a welfare dole. The "expert" is the teenager who is told to be a good boy but has as his next-door neighbors a prostitute and a junkie.

The impact of this program on the viewers, including this writer, was significant. It is not hard to identify with the terror of a small baby attacked in his bed by a rat. It is not difficult imaginatively to include oneself in the efforts of a family to find a decent place to live. When a show was produced demonstrating the mass of red tape and bureaucratic exploitation of the poor that are realities for the poverty-stricken, any middle-class person who ever tried to get even a little satisfaction from city hall appreciates their frustration. The consensus opinion of those who participated in this experiment in Christian education was that there was a far greater aura of reality in such shows as these than in most religious dramas, and certainly far more than one finds in the "gentle Jesus" stories of the Sunday school quarterlies.

Creative persons who are concerned about the ghetto of indifference in which we WASPs live and which separates us from the other Americans have tried, with some success, to reach the hearts of people by many art forms. With young people, especially college-age WASPs, much has been accomplished through the use of folk songs and folk singers. Prophets appear in strange costumes in our day, and young Christians may hear at least the message of social concern through a Bob Dylan or a Pete Seeger before they will listen to the best-intentioned message of the Rev. Whitecollar in First Church. Folk songs are often the heartfelt expression of people who have known poverty and discrimination and loneliness. Perhaps the reason for their current popularity is that they seem more real than either the sermons about compassion that are preached or the hymns written a hundred years ago which accompany them.

The implications for a church program of imaginative identification are more startling than they may seem on the surface. In addition to youth meetings in which young people talk about how to ask a girl for a date or the dangers of "following the crowd" (typical WASP concerns), there might also be a series of work camps in the slums of a nearby city, or a discussion about our responsibilities to the poor after a program of relevant folk songs. Instead of a social action committee simply arranging on a seldom-noticed table a few dusty pamphlets which state the most recent pronouncements of the denomination on race relations, this committee could arrange to have some deprived children spend a week of vacation in the affluent homes of the church members who are willing to open them. Rather than reading, always, "religious" literature in the name of the church, a bibliography might also include *Black Like Me,* the true story of a white man who dyed his skin black and learned firsthand what it meant to be a Negro in the South. Controversial? Undoubtedly, and this might be the first sign of hope.

Imagine, if you will, the women's groups studying *The Other America* by Michael Harrington and discussing it rather than, at best, just foreign missions, as important as this is, or, at worst, flower arranging and table decorations. Could not Negro churches and white churches worship together on Sunday evenings and, better yet, have a shared, cooperative supper before or after the service? The ways in which individual churches and individual Christians can work at exposing poor *people* and different colored people to WASP people are many, but they simply are seldom tried. At first, only a few will respond. Possibly the number will never grow very much.

Nevertheless, the present token efforts of most white Protestant churches in the area of human relations is simply not enough. We are only human, and we can scarcely be expected to love those we cannot see, or feel compassion for those who are only mysterious nonentities, or even vote for the legislation which may help those we do not understand.

Unless we become able imaginatively to identify with the have-nots, our best-laid plans and our most moving sermons will fall on deaf ears. Just as we must expose ourselves in twentieth-century terms to the fact that we are sinners in twentieth-century ways before we will want to change, so we will have to expose ourselves to the real *people* of other America—people who bleed and suffer and die, partly because of our own indifference. There is no guarantee that any of our efforts to come into contact with the have-nots will generate genuine compassion for them or a feeling for their causes; but this much is certain: *we will never be able to care very much for a figment of an affluent imagination. We are called to love human beings, not illusions.* "Traditional Protestant moralism is still one of our biggest problems," says Ted McIvenna of a Methodist inner-city project in San Francisco, the Glide Urban Center. "Oh, if we could hear the last of those time-honored sayings, 'A bad apple spoils the barrel,' and 'You don't have to climb into a cesspool to know it stinks.' Wouldn't it be lovely to recognize that people are neither apples nor cesspools?" [1]

[1] Carol D. Muller, "Engaging the City—With Love," *Together*, May, 1965, p. 18.

Actually, much of the main thrust of the Christian gospel has always been in the form of imaginative identification. We are asked to see people in new ways when we become Christian; we are asked to see them as part of the body of Christ. Kathryn Hulme illustrated this in her novel, *The Nun's Story*, when she had the Mother Superior of the hospital in which Sister Luke began her nursing career instruct the beginning nurses: *"All for Jesus. . . .* Say it, my dear students, every time you are called upon for what seems an impossible task. Then you can do anything with serenity. . . . Say it for the bedpans you carry, for the old incontinents you bathe, for those sputum cups of the tubercular." Then, as the Mother Superior bent over a patient to change a dressing foul with corruption, she said to the sisters in charge, "You see how easy? All for Jesus . . . this is no body picked up in the Rue des Radis. This is the Body of Christ and this suppurating sore is one of His Wounds." [2]

Before we will be able to generate concern and love for the least of these, we will have to discover that they are hungry and thirsty and naked and sick and in prison. If we can learn this much, maybe we will be compelled by a compassionate spirit to do something for people who once were strangers to us but have always been part of the body of Christ.

[2] (Boston: Little, Brown and Company, 1956), pp. 14-15.

THE CHRISTIAN
SCHIZOPHRENIC

4

One group of Christians found itself with an opportunity to break out of the ghetto of indifference. Sadly, how they reacted is not uncommon.

A group of Presbyterian elders who were also realtors in a Pittsburgh community were asked by their pastor to open the way for a cultured Negro family to purchase a home in their neighborhood. After a lengthy discussion in which they consulted Scripture, prayed and generally agonized over a decision, they summoned their minister and reported: "Our duty is clear. We know that as Christian men we ought to give the word that would make it possible for this man to find a house here, but God help us, we cannot do it. Most of us have spent a life time building up our businesses. The reprisals from the realty board, the banks, and certain other groups would be more than we could take and stay in business. Not only our businesses but our families would suffer all kinds of threats and social ostracism. We just can't do what we ought to do as Christians." [1]

Maintaining segregated patterns of housing is just one of the ways that the haves have rejected the have-nots. There are, of course, many others, but this particu-

[1] Gayraud S. Wilmore, *The Secular Relevance of the Church* (Philadelphia: The Westminster Press, 1962) , p. 49-50.

lar incident illustrates both the problem and an insight into a solution.

There is a misunderstanding of the nature of Christian vocation which causes much of our trouble, especially when we think of it in terms of the relationships between the rich and the poor, the white man and the Negro, or the persons in power and those who have been essentially disenfranchised. There seems to be the feeling that one cannot live in two worlds at the same time. As WASPs look at the television screen and newspaper accounts of, say, a civil rights demonstration, their eyes eventually rest on some of the participants who seem to be peculiar. Inevitably, they will see some who will be wearing long hair, sunglasses, beards, and dirty white sneakers. They will be singing, "We Shall Overcome," and middle-class man will look away with a small shudder and possibly reject the entire movement in revulsion. The beatniks may be nothing more than an excuse for not wanting to support such a movement, but many of us who do support such causes somehow, somewhere along the line, usually end up "explaining" the fact of their habitual presence. However, the point is that there is an assumption that one almost literally has to give up his complete way of life in order to be concerned with the have-nots. One has to become a beatnik or, at least, a social worker in the slums before he can get involved in the other America. He has to be some kind of "professional" Christian, specially trained to deal with the problems of other America. Like the rich young ruler who came to Jesus, asking what he had yet to do to be saved, a concerned, compassionate WASP may turn away sorrowing, knowing that he cannot give up his whole way of life for the have-nots.

Certainly there is a desperate need for those who are called to full-time work among the have-nots. Christian social workers who can resist the built-in hazard of cynicism that affects so many of that profession are desperately needed. Ministers in the inner-city, men and women living on the edge of a world where the problems are the keenest, are in short supply. Ministers who have caught the vision of the local church as an outpost in the service of all men regardless of race or economic circumstances cannot get to the local churches fast enough. To those who are called to such full-time vocations, there is but one word: Hurry! Christians are needed now as leaders in the full-time civil rights movement, and we dare not discount the kind of dedicated leadership we depend upon so fully.

However, our need for Christian schizophrenics is equally as great. Our need for men and women who are themselves affluent to some degree, who are probably white, who probably are Protestant, and who will live in two worlds at the same time is also desperate. It is abundantly apparent that there is a great shortage of haves, dwelling within middle-class society, who still have a concern for the have-nots. Our contemporary emphasis on the work of the laity in and through the church has sometimes been watered down into thinking that to be a practicing Christian merely requires that one be honest, have a worthwhile job that makes a positive contribution to society, talk to people about Christ on coffee breaks, and use his leisure time with profit for the Kingdom. All of this is part of the definition. However, in our day and in the knowledge of the ghetto of indifference which has trapped so many of us and which has been a plague on all our houses of worship, the definition will necessarily have to include another factor—a genuine desire to be Christian schizophrenics.

It means to share a genuine concern for the have-nots while simultaneously feeling it for the haves. It means a willingness to use our affluence or our place in the power structure or our very status as individual WASPs for the sake of the other Americans. The Christian realtor (re the example above) will have to say "yes" instead of "no," even if the "no" carries an apology. So often we have heard, in civil rights crises, the cry from WASPs that direct action is not the "best way." This is absolutely true. It is not the best way to achieve justice, but it is the only way simply because not enough of us have had the willingness and the courage to work for this particular group of have-nots from within the power structure.

How frustrated social workers must get as they seek to cut through red tape and outer offices of local bureaucracies only to get the run-around from a building inspector or a fire marshall or a health inspector.

Yet, how important the witness of men such as these would be to the Christian cause of concern for the children of God who are born in a tenement. Or, how helpful a Christian businessman could be if he took the time to say a word to the inspector or possibly even hint that he may speak a word to "his good friend, the mayor, about the whole situation." Robert W. Spike, director of the National Council of Churches Commission on Religion and Race, pointed out recently that if "congregations would really take the lead toward open housing, the problem could virtually be licked in five years' time." [2]

Business has often stood aloof from the racial crisis until it threatened them economically. In Little Rock the city had to undergo a serious financial setback before top business leaders took action against the defiance of Governor Faubus. In Virginia businessmen finally played a role in defeating "massive resistance" to school integration when the schools were closed and people began to leave the state. In Georgia, Mississippi, and Alabama businessmen took the reins from the hands of the extremists only when New York banks began to shy away from investments in their area. When finally businesses acted—and by businesses we mean persons who make decisions—it made a great and positive difference in the reaction of the general public. But why did it have to become an economic necessity before action took place?

[2] Robert S. Spike, "Our Churches' Sin Against the Negro," *Look Magazine*, May 18, 1965, p. 31.

Many of the southern businessmen involved would boast of their church backgrounds and family church relationships and the many fine organizations to which they belong. Yet they seemed unable to escape from the provincial kind of Christianity which exists in so many local communities.

True, there are some respectable churchgoing businessmen who make a living by exploiting the poor or the minorities, and it will take more than a word or a hint to get through to them. Nor should direct action be stopped in the hope that "someday" the haves will have a change of heart. It will probably be necessary for a long, long time to take such steps as one group of activists in Chicago has been doing. This group dispatches pickets to a slum landlord's neat and attractive neighborhood, and they march around with signs that say, "Did you know that one of Your neighbors is a Slum Lord? His name is. . . . He owns a dump at. . . . He refuses to conform to the standards of decency and live up to his responsibility. This is how he makes his money.[3]

However, WASP churches are not well-equipped for, nor psychologically oriented toward, this kind of forceful action. The most creative witness that Christian church members can make is to channel their goodwill (if it can be inspired) and their guilt (if it can be

[3] For a thorough discussion of the group in Chicago and those in other areas see Lyle Schaller, *Community Organization: Conflict and Reconciliation* (Nashville: Abingdon Press, 1966).

shown) into positive action for the sake of the other Americans. When once we see our own sinfulness and when once we feel compassion for real people, then our task comes to be one of strategy. *How* do we live in one world for the sake, at least partly, of another? How can I—a doctor, a lawyer, a businessman, a merchant, a housewife, a working man, or a farmer—get involved in the cause of mankind? How can we, as a local church on the corner, most effectively share in the ministry of the haves among the have-nots.

One of the first steps is to convince ourselves—possibly reconvince ourselves—of the power of individual witness and the influence which one or two people can have who are willing to take a stand. We need to be reminded of Frances Willard's familiar statement: "I am but one, but I am one; I cannot do much, but I can do something; what I can do, I ought to do; and what I ought to do, by the Grace of God I will do."

We have come to the point in this country wherein we assume we must represent a certain number of votes or a large amount of money or even an entire church before anything can be done. We would be naïve if we said that these facts of life are not important and that all we need to do is ride up on our white horses and the dragons will faint. This certainly is not the case, but neither is it the case that we are helpless prisoners of a corrupt society who can't ever fight city hall and must be content to sit the rest of our days, wringing our hands and sighing nostalgically for those times when knighthood was in flower.

Too many significant acts of individual witness have already taken place which disprove a belief in the bondage of the individual. Many individual WASPS have become Christian schizophrenics in one way or another, and they have won some personal battles even though the war does not always seem to be going their way. There is the Christian family which "adopted" a high school alcoholic and stood by her and with her all the way through college. Anyone who is familiar with the special problems and frustrations of alcoholism will understand the depth of commitment to a person that such devotion demands. These people, good Presbyterians and community leaders, are aware of the need to live in two worlds at the same time.

Or there comes to mind the sophisticated and charming woman who knows her way around a tea table but who has gone on a regular basis to help a forgotten family in a slum neighborhood, not just with charity, but with knowledge and guidance and genuine concern. Enlisting the aid of some of her friends who themselves were totally unfamiliar with life in the slums, her continuing relationship has included housecleaning, guidance in grocery shopping, direction in medical care, and help to get the children into an understanding Sunday school. This is a big step beyond the Christmas basket approach and becomes a small-scale welfare operation—at no government expense!

Or one thinks of the school teacher who applied to a school system, asking if there would be any opportunity to teach the disadvantaged child. She was a college beauty queen who sought to move from one world to another and back again. Her idealism came from her Christian concern for people as children of God, and her request prompted one school-board member to exclaim, "Usually the place where she wanted to teach is regarded as the Siberia of the school system!" This is Christian schizophrenia.

We could include, too, the young women who went twice a month to a settlement house in one community and taught the backward mothers of that area how to wash their babies and sew clothes and live on a budget. Contrary to many common fears about such activity, their own families were not neglected, their own values were not distorted, and no infectious diseases were caught or transmitted.

Or picture in your mind a civil rights march in a mid-western city, led neither by the beatniks nor by the preachers nor by the professional civil rights workers, but by one of the most respected (and wealthy) family physicians of that city. Add to this impression the image of the realtor who went quietly—and with some success —to other members of the board of realtors, working for an open-housing policy. Include in your picture the attorney who specializes in the cases of the have-nots, yet who also has plenty of business from the haves.

He just happens to be an excellent attorney and an excellent Christian at the same time.

It has been interesting to note, furthermore, the sense of genuine relief which several WASPs expressed when their community became involved in the Project Head Start program, the government effort to help prepare kindergarten-age children from underprivileged and semi-illiterate homes for entering school in the fall. This gave them a chance to serve, for while professional teachers were hired for the major teaching responsibilities, there were a number of volunteer assistants needed for such tasks as giving the children two meals a day plus soap and water and medical care.

Do not discount the achievements of a charming and delightful lady in North Carolina who was a member of the school board when her city took the lead in the integration of schools in that state. Was it merely a coincidence that she was also a dedicated and concerned Christian woman? We think also of the dean of one of this country's foremost universities who just recently had to give up a private service of tutoring underprivileged Negro children because of the tremendous press of professional responsibilities. Still, however, his feelings and his heart function with two worlds in mind. Do not fail to remember the high school music teacher who gave up his vacation to go to Chicago to work in a slum neighborhood with Negro children, teaching them to read and write and also demonstrating that there are some who care out in the white world beyond the tenements. Do not omit the Christian schizophrenics who serve as voluntary probation officers for delinquent boys and girls, or those remarkable men and women who give their time in many cities teaching slum children how to sew or work with their hands. Such Christians as these live in two worlds at the same time. They move freely between them. They are not bound by the walls of a ghetto of indifference.

Think, if you will, of the kind of impact these collective experiences would make if only a few individuals in a single city took their example seriously! Coming as they do from a variety of geographical sources, they may only represent a little witness in the face of big problems. However, they are worth something in and of themselves, at least to the child who learns to read, the Negro who finds a decent home in which to live, and the family which begins to have hope. Equally important is the fact that they illustrate that haves can and do move between both worlds. Most important of all, however, is the effect such actions have in changing the attitudes of other WASPs toward the poor and disenfranchised. Americans live in a society which has the capability, technically, to abolish poverty and the machinery, politically, to eliminate discrimination. However, it is open to debate whether it is a society *morally* capable of doing so. The witness of individual Christians is part of the nurture of the social morality necessary to make the big changes which are yet to come.

Right now the number of individuals who are genuine Christian schizophrenics is small. When we contrast the hope and the encouragement offered by the few witnessing WASPs with the number of churches having 500 or a 1,000 or more members who are not even producing a single Christian living in both worlds, the picture is not bright. This sight makes us want to cry out in anger and frustration. Yet, we do not need to wait until all the other 999 or our 1,000-member church agree with us on a course of action. That day may never come. City hall can be visited by one person. A family in the slums can become a place for help and for love to be expressed. The right word in the right ear expressed in the right manner by the right person can help build a bridge between two worlds.

Assuming that the local church is willing to co-operate and help individuals in these efforts—at times, a rather hopeful assumption—there will have to be a different approach to much of its program than now exists. There is little doubt that individuals—and groups of individuals—would get more involved in the needs of the other America if local churches would provide more realistic opportunities for them to do so. Many WASPs have good intentions and the momentum to get involved, but they feel insecure about how to go about getting the job done. The individuals we men-tioned above had both the courage to do something as well as a practical approach in mind. Our concern in the local church ought to be like their individual concerns—first to raise the issues and then provide a strategy.

Our world is complex and city hall is frightening. Politics is a mysterious business to most Americans and probably especially so to the WASP whose whole church experience has emphasized the importance of avoiding sin and corruption in his personal life—and "everyone knows politics is dirty." Thus, the program of the local church is going to have to be changed, even radically changed at times, to help the individual Christians who seek to break out of their ghetto of indifference. Present efforts to get the church into the world are often viewed as experiments, but they may well foretell the kind of program that the local church will have to adopt if its concern for the world is to be translated into action. Most informed Christians are familiar with inner-city projects such as the East Harlem Protestant Parish in New York City or the Detroit Industrial Mission. In metropolitan areas such as the ones these projects serve, parish churches can learn much from them for their own programs.

George D. Younger, in his book *The Church and Urban Power Structure,* tells how some alert churches are urging and preparing their members for participation in the political life of their cities. He comments:

Eschewing the crusade approach that would descend upon the city's political parties as the knight in shining armor determined to rescue the urban maiden from the toils of the politicians, these Christians have studied carefully the political structure of their area, chosen their party, and then moved into it at the local level of precinct or election district, where the basic work of political organization is done. . . . By laying claim to politics as a sphere of Christian ministry, they show that they are not content with the present situation where the churches are expected to leave business to businessmen and politics to the politicians. They also demonstrate that the work of God can be done through politics as through all the other spheres of city life.[4]

It is through politics that much can be done to help the have-nots on a large scale, since so often the people who man the various political offices that affect the lot of the poor and disadvantaged are simply political hacks who have little genuine sympathy for the outcasts of society. Political understanding as to how these important appointments are made can be part of the wisdom of serpents put to use by some Christian doves. A few politically astute Christian women simply entered upon a small letter-writing effort in one city, encouraging the circuit court judge to appoint a certain person to the county welfare department in whom they had confidence as to his personal sensitivity and fairness. The "right" man was appointed, and who knows to what degree these women influenced the judge's decision. Knowing the pecking order of a bureaucracy will give guidance to the persons who seek to bring about some social

[4] (Philadelphia: The Westminster Press, 1963), pp. 78-79.

changes in favor of the ones who need them the most. There are denominational leaders and some men in public life who can provide the leadership for such a program if the local church takes its new responsibilities seriously and faces the world realistically.

One group of salesmen from the Church of Our Savior in West Bloomfield, Michigan, called upon the leadership of the Detroit Industrial Mission to help them with a course in the relationship of the Christian faith to what they deal with on the job. The assumptions which the leader of the group made about the classes might well be taken seriously by others in local churches, especially when we consider the clear relationship between the industrial world and the invisible Americans. The leader, Jim Campbell, said this:

I assume you are the missionaries in today's world. But you're not "converting" people in the old sense. You're not carrying a bundle of pre-packaged truth, rules, or principles to dump on others. Rather, you are a catalyst (thermostat!) of discussion and action about the kinds of issues and concerns we've been kicking around in this series. You're an organization man trying your damnedest to shape that organization so it's fit for those in it (including yourselves), those touched by it, and the society it serves.

Your allies in this are not necessarily other churchmen. God uses all kinds of people for his purposes. So there's no place for religious arrogance or "holier than thou." Your allies are people who share at least some of your concerns and goals for the organization, profession, or occupation you are in.[5]

Churches and individual Christians are going to have to change some of their thinking, too, about who their enemies and their allies are in the modern battle with evil. Instead of competing with other agencies in the community for time, we will have to cooperate with such groups as the welfare board, the YMCA, the Mental Health Association, the probation officer, the school system, and many other agencies in a planned and conscious effort to deal with many of the social and moral problems which plague both the haves and the have-nots. Gordon Cosby puts it this way:

The shape of the church will be determined in large measure by the world. . . . Christ made himself vulnerable to the world. The church is to be vulnerable to the world. It is to take the shape the world needs. We are not to be protected by our own power structures which are so strong that the world cannot crucify us.

From time to time whole churches, or at least groups acting in the name of the church under their own power and on their own initiative, can move into the other America with direct action programs and projects. Realistically speaking, this will not happen as often as it should, for many times the power structures of a local congregation think primarily in terms of per-

[5] "Life and Work," Bulletin of The Detroit Industrial Mission, VII (Spring, 1965).

petuating the institution rather than furthering the kingdom of God. Nevertheless, it is more than just possible *theoretically*. Some churches have left their ghetto *as churches,* and others could very well imitate them.

One congregation carries on a continuing nursery school for children from a slum area. Another opened a study room in an area where there was no record of any child having ever graduated from high school, partly because there was no quiet place to study or any adult around to keep order. Robert Raines tells of another experiment in one Ohio church which has been called, appropriately, "The Outpost."

The Outpost would be a center of information for both urban and suburban communities, concerning such problems as employment, education, welfare, urban renewal, political action, volunteer community programs—Boy Scouts, United Appeal, etc.—hospitals and clinics, housing, alcoholism, and juvenile delinquency. It would also provide suitable facilities for the collection of food and used clothing for city churches and materials for Goodwill Industries, or a secretarial service to urban and suburban churches, for a meeting place for noon prayer groups and other interdenominational groups, and for an outlet for the products of the home industries of members of city churches.[6]

Another group of churchmen started a program in cooperation with the local probation officer in which the men would direct and work on certain projects of

[6] *Reshaping the Christian Life* (New York: Harper & Row, 1964), p. 59.

hard physical labor along with some juvenile offenders who had been in trouble with the law. The impact on the boys when they worked alongside businessmen, school teachers, and others was significant, and an attitude was changed in the minds of some about the dignity of physical work. Some felt it was not so "square" after all. Creative Christians are capable of many other projects which will help build the bridge from one world to another. It can be done, and the realization that it is possible will necessarily precede the concrete and practical methods of getting the job done. A WASP vice-virtue which ought to be taken seriously is the self-reliance that a way at the local level *can be found.*

It is important to emphasize, too, that there is a basic connection between the total work of a local church and the specific work of outreach to the have-nots. The local church, as such, will never be as radical as a civil rights movement and never quite as concerned about people "over there" as it ought to be for the obvious reason that it is *both* a priestly *and* a prophetic community. In other words it seeks to be an agent which helps people with personal problems as well as dealing with the social needs of a city or town. It seeks to provide a ministry and be a redemptive fellowship for the sick, the lonely, the anxiety-ridden, and the bereaved. There are within most congregations many individuals who don't care about the poor or the Negroes or anybody else because they are all wrapped up in themselves. When a marriage is breaking up, the participants will scarcely be very concerned about race relations. When a family is suffering through a long and self-draining bedside vigil of a loved one, it seldom worries much about the demoralizing conditions of the slums. The local church is fighting many battles at the same time.

Thus, it is important that we see the connection between the priestly work of the practicing Christian and his prophetic witness. The local church has to do both, and the neglect of one will affect the other. Ministers owe as much concern to the enrolled bigots of their congregations as they do to the unenrolled poor on the other side of the tracks. Often the young man or woman who is willing, even eager, to march in a demonstration will completely overlook an opportunity to visit a segregationist in a hospital. Indeed, one can sympathize with the pastor of a suburban church who has done a great deal to lead his congregation out of their WASP ghetto who said this in a personal letter:

I get a little tired of the professional critics of the local church who are always telling us how much we have failed. God knows how much we've failed, and so do I. But I sometimes want to ask the professional social actionist how many bedsides he visited that day, how many marriages he tried to save, and how many neurotic women he confronted with the Gospel of Jesus Christ.

Because of this particular minister's obvious efforts on behalf of the have-nots, what he says can be viewed as more than a mere rationalization. Furthermore, it shows us an important insight into a fact which the local church has to take seriously at all times. The very nature of the Christian community will slow it down, but the strategy of a local church ought to be built upon the premise that love for people who are sick is of the same essential stuff as love for the poverty-stricken. Both share in the *agape,* the Christian love, which is the goal, at least, of Christian people as they live their daily lives. There is reason to believe that if more church members functioned as ministers and counselors to one another, more of them would function as ministers-at-large in the world. WASPs who don't understand "those people" in the slums or the Negro ghetto or in the nearby migrant camp may understand, however, that the feelings they had for a fellow church member who was dying of cancer are like the feelings their minister or some other Christians often feel for the have-nots. Possibly the quality of a person who spends his Saturdays working with underprivileged children will influence a tenement owner somewhat, too, if he spends one Saturday visiting him. Christian persons, and especially ministers, are sometimes guilty of irresponsible moralizing, telling people how to behave while failing to demonstrate a spirit of fellowship and compassion for the "sinners" they confront.

The Christian whose base of operations is the local church is seldom allowed the luxury of being a specialist. He will have strengths and weaknesses which will enable him to function in some areas of the church's work better than others. Some will spend more time helping couples with their marital problems than they will spend working with kids on probation from the court. And vice versa. However, unlike the Negro civil rights worker or the professional social worker, the white, middle-class American is not his natural "enemy" or opponent. He is part of WASP-land, yet critical of it. He looks at himself and he knows the temptations to self-righteousness which have conquered many decent Christians and have helped build the walls of the WASP ghettos. He is both part of the problem and part of the solution.

We who are white, middle-class, and Protestant do not necessarily have to become poverty-stricken for the sake of the poor. It is not only permissible but recommended that we read good books and go to the opera and enjoy a family vacation in the Rockies—if we can afford it. Nevertheless, the Christian who cares in a genuine way for the have-nots of the world is not completely sane by the standards of our success-oriented culture. He still cares for "those people." He does all kinds of strange things for their sake that may cause him at least some inconveniences, frequently sums of money, and at most his very life. He is a schizophrenic, living in two worlds at the same time, demonstrating a kind of insanity which comes from following Another whom he calls, in faith, the living Christ.

In Dixon, Illinois, a few years ago, the local Church of the Brethren was in the process of constructing a new building. One morning it was discovered that some-one had smeared tar all over the inside and outside of the church, with an especially thorough job having been done on the cross which was on the front side of the building. Police were not sure who did this van-dalism or why it was done. Some speculated that it might have been done by labor renegades who were angry because the church had not been completely built with union labor. Or it could have been simply one of those senseless acts of violence which sometimes occur without any reasonable explanation. More than likely, however, the vandalism took place because the Brethren congregation had proposed to sell its old building to a congregation of Negro Baptists. At any rate, however, the reaction of the members of this church to the in-cident is significant. Speaking for them in a public statement the pastor said, "While I am sorry for the culprits, whoever they are, I am also grateful to them. This incident indicates that what the congregation stood for had registered with somebody, and therefore the tar on the cross is a badge of honor."

The popularity of the church in our day is probably the clearest indication of its failure to be the church of Jesus Christ. Most people in most communities are glad there are churches. It lends dignity and a sense of stability to have church buildings around, and it is nice to have ministers available for certain public functions such as weddings, funerals, and ground-breaking ceremonies. In this friendly, freedom-loving land the church belongs. Why not enjoy it?

However, if the local church takes seriously the fact of its responsibility to the have-nots of the world, it will cease to be just a comforting symbol and become, even more suddenly, a disturbing one. Any group of Christians who speak or act their convictions will eventually find themselves in trouble. Any individual Christian who involves his life to any significant degree in the lives of "undesirables" will soon drop out of competition in a popularity contest. By being a priest as well as a prophet, he may be able to have his cake and eat it, too, for awhile, but eventually he can expect anonymous phone calls, personal insults, or possibly something even worse. When Christ said that he came, not to bring peace but a sword, this is undoubtedly part of what he meant.

It would be dishonest to suggest that one could break out of his ghetto of indifference for the sake of his neighbor in another ghetto without tension or trouble. It can't be done, or, if seemingly it can, one either lives in New Jerusalem or probably has not done all that he ought to do. Sarah Patton Boyle in her profound and moving book, *The Desegregated Heart,* describes how she had hoped that there would be some who would stand by her when she took her stand for freedom and justice for the Negro in her native state of Virginia. She hoped for support from the "liberals" she knew, but one by one they deserted her. She hoped for understanding from her intimate friends, but she found herself gradually socially ostracized. Surely the Negro community would stand by her, she felt, but years of suspicion and well-grounded mistrust overcame even that source of support. She stood alone with God and her convictions.

Few of us probably will suffer this fate, for persons who possess her degree of integrity and conviction are rare indeed. Even small adventures, however, bring small risks and sometimes at least a little tar is smeared on our personal crosses. One family which hosted a Negro child for two weeks in an all-white neighborhood discovered a jar of urine on its doorstep one morning. Others received anonymous phone calls. One family was temporarily ostracized by its neighbors. This writer learned in a tiny degree about personal degradation when a barber refused to cut his hair after cutting the hair of a Negro man he had accompanied to the shop. Another person who worked in a settlement house on a regular basis lost the tires off his car, stolen probably by some of the persons he was trying to help. Ministers may lose their pulpits. Churches are sometimes divided. Christians may lose their friends.

Realization that Christian witness will bring trouble may be one of the main dissuading factors in our failing to act our convictions. Perhaps more WASPS than not realize they are asking for trouble, and perhaps it is time that we recognize a special kind of courage reserved for the haves when they extend a hand to the have-nots. The WASPS have something to lose—property, community position, commercial business, friendship, or peace of mind. Because they have more to lose, their courage in small ways may at times be comparable to that of the free-wheeling college student risking his neck in a civil rights demonstration or a professional social worker spending his life working in the slums. The WASPS are not free agents, and the call to stand up and be counted is often more difficult to answer when one is among friends than when he is among enemies, or at least among people who don't care much one way or another. The church-going middle class holds great power in its hands, so far as our social revolution is concerned. If its members use it wisely and determinedly, they can still, even at this late date, change the world. Yet, let us not forget that a special kind of courage will be required.

The need for this special kind of Christian courage and integrity, however, ought not to be the most disturbing fact the WASPS face. More disturbing is the fact of general uneasiness which comes when we compare ourselves to those whose commitment to Christ, or to the least of his children, has cost them everything. Lou Marsh, a young member of the Youth Board in New York City, lost his life at the hands of a juvenile gang which was resentful of his positive influence among younger members of the group. He died, not for the freshly scrubbed, bright young faces of a church youth group such as yours or mine, but for a gang of tough kids who, if they are lucky, may one day stay out of prison part of the time. Or one reads the moving story of the East Harlem Protestant Parish in *Come Out the Wilderness* by Bruce Kendrick, and then he thinks of what he is doing and a vague feeling of uneasiness clouds his mind.

The Christian in a local church can do something. He can, he ought, and he must do more than he is now doing just to escape his ghetto. Still, he may wonder: "Is it enough? Where ought I to serve? What ought I to do?" If a special kind of courage is demanded of the WASP, a special kind of temptation is always with him as well, the temptation to do less than he is able and then justify his reticence. The great temptation he faces is that he will retire before his job is done. The men and women who have followed the way of Christ to the end have found continual dissatisfaction with themselves along the route. They have found there is always a second mile, always a new challenge, always a sense of uneasiness in knowing that, in spite of what they may have already done, Christ *still* calls "follow me."

Perhaps a parable will make this point clear.

It happened that some of the devil's most cunning tempters sought to capture for Hell a young Christian by the name of Arthur Dox. They tempted him with wine, women, and song—with no results. They tried bribery without success and completely failed in all other forms of personal corruption. Finally, in desperation, the tempters turned to Satan himself, to the Master of Misery, for guidance.

Fearfully, the tempters gathered at the feet of the Mighty One, ready for whatever blows or curses might come. To their surprise, however, he read their report rapidly and with no comment. Page after page was skimmed without a change in the pleasant snarl he wore on his face. Finally, with a grunt, he turned to the spokesman of the group and snapped: "Well, you miserable wretches, where is the rest of it?"

"The rest of what?" replied the cowering cowards, backing away.

"The rest of the report, you idiots!" he screamed.

"That's all, master," whined one tempter, dodging a kick from the Mighty One. "You've heard it all."

"No, no, no, you imbeciles. I don't care about all these silly plans of yours. What I want to know is the answer to the one crucial question about Arthur Dox that he and his kind must always answer for us. The essential question is: What is he wearing?"

"What is he wearing?" The tempters groaned in amazement. Had the old Beast lost his evil mind? No, that was impossible. Timidly, the spokesman answered: "The last we saw of him he had on a gray Harris Tweed jacket, a light-blue button-down shirt, a dark striped tie—such as a Yale man might wear—neatly tied in a half-Windsor knot, gray wool socks, all in all well-dressed when you consider that most of the editors of *Playboy* are down here. But, most damnable one, why do you want to know this?"

At this question a light appeared in his eyes that might have been interpreted as joy, had it not been so hateful. "Don't you see, you oafs, the man is still a bystander. He thinks in a reasonable manner. He is a nice guy. He is well behaved himself and he wants to live a good life. For these reasons he is not yet ours. But neither has he escaped us. His dress gives him away. He is still in the world and to a great extent of the world. His God has not yet captured him with fire and devotion. Nor has he shown himself ready to carry a cross, regardless of the persecution that will come to him. He is not yet ours; that is true. But neither is he God's.

"However, dear friends, keep your eyes on this man. For when the day comes that he is so devoted to the service of Him on High that he literally loses himself in the doing of his will, then he is lost to us. When he is so little concerned about himself that he goes about town in an old pin-striped suit, double-breasted, wearing a starched collar with a flowered tie, he has become a real threat to us. When his trousers lose their press and his shoes are scuffed, our cause is lost and he will have escaped our clutches."

With these words Satan dismissed his tempters. But somewhere, up on earth, Arthur Dox shivered almost as if he felt a pair of evil eyes watching his very soul.

If only he could know, if only all such as he could understand, that until man commits himself totally to the One on High, he is never out of reach of those who dwell below.

INDEX